it's come to this

it's come to this

A Pandemic Diary

Laura Pedersen

For permission requests: LauraPedersenBooks.com

ISBN: 978-1-7367362-0-3
E-ISBN: 978-1-7367362-1-0

Library of Congress Control Number: 2021904773

Cover and interior design by Tabitha Lahr

Printed in the United States of America

Hang on to your hat. Hang on to your hope.
And wind the clock, for tomorrow is another day.

—E.B. WHITE

I like France, where everybody thinks he's Napoleon—
down here everybody thinks he's Christ.
　　　　　—F. SCOTT FITZGERALD

Chapter 1

A Hot Time in Toulouse

A friend called and invited me to an F. Scott Fitzgerald conference a few years back. I assumed the conference was in Fitzgerald's birthplace of St. Paul, Minnesota, though it would've made sense if it were in Manhattan or Long Island, or even Alabama, where Fitzgerald famously courted his future wife Zelda.

"It's in Toulouse," my friend said.

"Toulouse?" I replied. "Where's that?" Of course, I know about Toulouse, France, but why would a Fitzgerald Conference be there? He explained that the host in Italy, where the Fitzgeralds actually lived for a time, had canceled at the last minute. France sounded good to me. A woman in my building was from the South of France, and her children left out wine for Santa and carrots for his reindeer.

Traveling to JFK airport from the Upper East Side should be a simple affair since it's only fifteen miles as the pigeon flies. Traffic is usually horrendous and for the sake of expediency and the environment, I prefer public transportation. From my front door I walked six blocks to the subway wearing a backpack and dragging a suitcase, since after the conference I planned on doing some sightseeing. This ten-minute walk required navigating entire blocks of scaffolding, construction workers having a sandwich or a smoke, tables operated by fruit vendors, double-wide baby carriages, tourists strolling three across, and pedestrians standing in the middle of the sidewalk transfixed by their phones.

Upon reaching the 86th Street subway station, I heaved my bag down two flights of stairs still slippery from a recent downpour. Upon reaching the bottom step I was fairly certain the mesh where I'd had a hernia operation five years earlier had ripped wide open. The platform was chockablock with irritable commuters, and the grunts and scowls made it clear that an overstuffed backpack and suitcase were not welcome. The crowd continued to grow exponentially and after a ten-minute wait I pushed my bags and myself inside a 6 train. No teen or twenty-something offered a seat to this fifty-something, so I took that as a compliment.

There's no direct public transport to the airport from Manhattan, the way there is in every civilized city around the globe, so at 53rd street it was necessary to switch to an E train. I had to walk down two flights of stairs because the escalator was broken, as is often the case with subway escalators. It was 90°F and humid on this early summer day, but there was no air-conditioning on the platform. I boarded the next train and listened to school children loudly debate whether you should think ahead before getting a tattoo or do it spontaneously, and who are the best artists. We were stalled for ten minutes between stations due to a track fire and those checking their phones for information couldn't get any reception.

At Sutphin Boulevard in Queens, I exited the train and lugged my bags for a mile, squeezed into a jam-packed elevator, rode up two levels, and searched for the airlink to JFK among several subway and bus lines. A detour steered me an additional half mile that traversed an outdoor bus lane where I passed a dozen homeless people and several panhandlers and felt horrible about traveling to France.

A long line snaked toward the row of turnstiles where it was necessary to reinsert my metro card. However, many travelers were angry to discover they had to pay another fare and refill their cards, which required standing in a different line. The turnstiles were locking for no apparent reason and agents in orange vests helped with mixed success.

After ninety minutes of sweating through my clothes and facing a possible groin rupture, I was on the Airlink to JFK. Six overhead signs in large orange letters asked, FEELING ILL? THINK IT'S A COLD? IT COULD BE MEASLES. Once again, I wasn't nearly as excited about a trip to France as I had been that morning.

I arrived at Terminal 8 and it was a mere mile to the check-in counter. Unprovoked, the ticket agent informed me that if I paid to use the lounge, there was a shower. It's worth noting that what I just described is the *best* public transportation option available from the Upper East Side to JFK. I was not in training for any athletic events, purposely seeking hardship, or trying to economize—I just didn't want to be stuck in traffic for two hours in ninety-degree heat while trapped inside a taxi with a plexiglass barrier that insured air-conditioning for the driver and a sauna for the passenger. Still, the only reason I lived to tell the public transportation story is because I'm in relatively good shape and traveling solo, whereas a senior citizen, or someone with a child, or a person with the slightest disability would have been severely challenged. I wondered why going to the airport was an Olympic event, or else a contest for those who are bored with Tough Mudder endurance races, which feature obstacles that "play on common human fears, such as fire, water, electricity, and heights"—check, check, check, and check.

Toulouse is an elegant, historic city in Southern France perched on the banks of the glorious River Garonne, without all the grittiness and pickpockets of Marseilles. A day before leaving I'd checked the weather to have just the right attire for the end of June. I'm accustomed to the Fahrenheit temperature scale, however, when I was in elementary school there was a big push to learn the metric system. Supposedly we were all going to convert at any moment, like the countries that changed from driving on the left-hand side of the road to the right-hand side in a single day. As a result, I spent most of my youth multiplying by one and eight tenths and adding thirty-two. Low and behold, the Celsius switcheroo never came to pass, and we've been accidentally blowing things up ever since due to calculation errors. Nevertheless, the Great Metric Scare familiarized me with the system, and it was useful for ordering Loganberry by the liter and fireworks by the kilo in Canada. So when I'd read that Toulouse was supposed to be 108 degrees, I thought that was odd, since metric temperatures are considerably *below* their Fahrenheit counterpart. One hundred eight? I decided that France must have switched to an even newer form of measurement, perhaps based on a carafe of wine or the length of a baguette. However, a little Googling revealed that the duration of my trip would be accompanied by a "Sahara Desert heat wave" and that 108 was indeed Fahrenheit.

Being from Buffalo, I know all about weird weather, including lake-effect snow, thundersnow, Alberta clippers, ground blizzards, the slightly pornographic-sounding large scale frontal blizzard, and since moving to New York City, I've added Manhattan trash twisters to the list. Yet, I still don't know the cause or even the definition of a Sahara Desert heat wave other than to say it was 107°F, humid, *and* windy—WTF?

Upon arrival I discovered that Toulousians weren't in the habit of functioning at the broiling level either. Few stores had air-conditioning and thus vegetables wilted on the shelf and soap bars melted in their boxes while jam, chocolate mousse, and candy dissolved into sticky puddles. But just like Buffalo snowstorms, this bizarre weather system didn't keep residents inside.

The difference is that in Toulouse people seem to leave the house at the exact same time, as if a bell chimed in the town square. From seven until ten at night the entire city is out dining, promenading, and bar hopping while kids play in fountains or skate outside the Capitol Building, whereas in Manhattan it feels more like everyone has a time slot—school-age children dominate the streets from 3 to 5 p.m., seniors from 5 to 7 p.m., middle agers from 7 to 11 p.m., and then the young adults take over until the clubs close down.

What impressed me the most was the quality and ubiquity of pizza, which I associate with Italy rather than France. The only complaint I heard among visiting Americans was that enjoying this delicious pizza requires sitting down at a table and waiting ten minutes to have your order taken, and then another twenty minutes for the pizza, which is an entire pie, when you only wanted a slice or two, and have to be someplace in ten minutes. I understand the French way is to slow down and savor life. And I plan on doing this if Socialist Bernie Sanders is ever elected President, abolishes student debt, gives everyone free health care, and rebuilds our collapsing infrastructure. Until then we need to keep turning those tables, and New Yorkers like to incorporate eating into whatever else they happen to be doing.

Based on all the fruit and vegetable stalls lining the streets, it should be simple to find vegetarian meals in France. While I didn't see any cows or chickens in the streets, cheese and pastry shops are everywhere. At Senor Taco on my way to the metro station, I sat down at a table and ordered a vegetarian burrito in my best menu French. The waiter waved his finger saying, "*Non!*"—burritos were only to go. If I wanted to dine at a table, I had to order tacos. Oddly, I heard a young man from Ireland engaged in a similar dialogue with his waiter. When the waiters departed with our taco orders we conferred and found no reason why burritos shouldn't be consumed inside the restaurant. It felt like a famous *Saturday Night Live* sketch from my youth where the Olympia Restaurant served only cheeseburgers and Pepsi.

At the F. Scott Fitzgerald conference, I met a medievalist named Liam. He was an experienced academic conference-goer, whereas this was my first time. I asked if medievalist gatherings featured any jousting. He said there used to be fun stuff like that at the big annual conference in Kalamazoo but no longer. Having been a camp counselor for several years, and recalling a human pyramid in a rowboat that ended badly for the children and the rowboat alike, I sensed a story.

"What happened?" I asked.

Liam sighed wistfully and mysteriously replied, "a trebuchet." He proceeded to recount how the medievalists spent several days building a powerful siege catapult with a swinging arm that launches projectiles. For the demonstration a watermelon was employed as the projectile, and in front of several hundred spectators it shot through the air and destroyed a parked Volkswagen. I guessed they didn't have any physicists on the team. I told Liam not to feel bad—that I live a block from Frank Lloyd Wright's Guggenheim Museum and it's always falling down, so even the most creative minds often skip past the engineering component.

Back in Paris I toured Père Lachaise Cemetery, where numerous famous figures are buried, including Marcel Proust, Maria Callas, and Sarah Bernhardt. Colette and Edith Piaf have many visitors who are ardent admirers—mementos are carefully placed on the concrete slabs. In comparison, some fans of Jim Morrison and Oscar Wilde are vandals in the extreme, which has resulted in those monuments being cordoned off, yet worshippers still manage to defile them with lipstick and graffiti. When it comes to cemetery visits, Americans seem to land somewhere between the two extremes. F. Scott Fitzgerald's grave at St. Mary's in Rockville is open to the public and unguarded. Admirers leave notes and flowers and liquor bottles—especially liquor bottles, empty and full, but I've not witnessed any desecration.

I very much wanted the French to like me and not view me as an Ugly American. When working on projects with French colleagues, I've found them delightful, likewise when visiting friends in France. Thus, I threw myself out there with my best high school French from forty years ago. For instance, what came out as "Please telephone for the marching at seven early" meant I'd like a wake-up call. Despite my best efforts, I found the people in most sectors of the hospitality industry to be scowly, disinterested, and unhelpful. While discussing my experience with a tour guide (is it *me*?), he said the government recently sent out a memo demanding hoteliers, waiters, cabbies, and basically everyone interfacing with tourists be nicer to visitors. I'm not sure I believe him, but there's a chance that "Surly French" will become as ubiquitous as "Ugly American." I can understand being a cranky French farmer or even shopkeeper, but a bus driver who hates tourists seems arduous all around, like a flight attendant who hates flying.

When it was time to leave, I walked two blocks from my hotel to the nearest metro station, where, despite the outside heat, the platform was a comfortable temperature. Likewise, inside the train it was not steaming or freezing. After one simple change of trains that included a working escalator, I arrived at my airport terminal in no need of a shower. I could only conclude that purposely employing crotchety service providers was the secret to France's superior mass transit system.

A month after the conference in Toulouse, I asked the location of the next one and was told, "Jacksonville." Unaware of any affiliation between Fitzgerald and Jacksonville, Florida, I once again inquired, "Where is that?" Indeed, unbeknownst to me, Fitzgerald had apparently once stayed a few days at a hotel in a Jacksonville. I asked why the conference had never been held in Buffalo, since that's where Fitzgerald spent more years than anywhere else, albeit when he was young. Furthermore, Buffalo had numerous sights in synch with the modernism that the Jazz Age bard explored in his writing—the Pierce-Arrow Museum, Twentieth Century Club (where he took dancing lessons), the Albright-Knox Art Gallery, and edifices by the era's most famous architects including Frank Lloyd Wright, H.H. Richardson, and Louis Sullivan.

The organizer asked, "Do you know someone?" Indeed, I did, and promised to get some room rates. After a few phone calls it transpired that the next conference would be in Buffalo! But that was all B.C.—Before Coronavirus.

It was an uncertain spring.

—Virginia Woolf,

Chapter 2

Once in a Lifetime

There was a day in October of 1987, when the bears on Wall Street decidedly outmaneuvered the bulls, that I automatically assumed would be the worst experience of my life. As a twenty-two-year-old trader on the floor of the stock exchange, I was trampled by brokers with sell orders while the Dow Jones plummeted 22.6 percent in a single session, at that time the largest one-day drop in history. Panic reverberated around the world as investors tried to unload their entire portfolios instantaneously, while no buyers could be found at almost any price. Bank accounts were emptied. Livelihoods went up in smoke. There were suicides and murders. After losing millions, one distraught investor shot two Merrill Lynch executives and then took his own life.

Nevertheless, I turned out to be incorrect about Black Monday being the worst day of my life. Fourteen years down the track, the 9/11 terrorist attacks occurred on an otherwise perfect autumn morning. This would surely be the defining tragedy of my existence—The Big One—when planes slammed into the World Trade Center, buildings collapsed, a mushroom cloud of ominous black smoke engulfed lower Manhattan, trapped workers leapt to their deaths, and we searched for loved ones amidst the rubble but still lost an unbearable number of lives. Having worked nearby, many of the victims were good friends and former flames. Signs with photos were posted on buildings, mailboxes, and lampposts asking, "Have you seen So and So?" which left passersby shocked and unsettled, as if people were lost pets. Every evening at sunset, groups would gather near West Street to cheer the brave and tireless police, firefighters, demolition workers, and chaplains.

Eleven years later, in October of 2012, Superstorm Sandy came barreling off the Atlantic. This Category 3 hurricane took at least seventy-two lives, destroyed 650,000 homes, inflicted over $70 billion in damage, and made it quite clear that Manhattan could be sent packing by a single left hook from Mother Nature. A stage play I'd written was running at a downtown theater while my lead actor remained stranded in Hoboken amidst the rising waters. Newscasters said Superstorm Sandy was a "one-hundred-year event," only it felt as if we were hearing that expression rather regularly with regard to hurricanes, cyclones, earthquakes, avalanches, tsunamis, tornadoes, typhoons, heat waves, deep freezes, and wildfires.

Fast forward to January of 2020. The year began normally enough, with hundreds of thousands of people standing shoulder-to-shoulder in Times Square counting down as the ball dropped and firework displays erupted around the city. New Yorkers were hopeful; the economy was good and there'd be an election. Our resolutions were quaint—go to the gym more, spend less, and learn a language using one of those computer programs. Little did we suspect that something deadly was already in the air we were breathing that fateful New Year's Eve.

It was said to have originated at a live animal market in Wuhan, China, perhaps from a pangolin, a scaly mammal that resembles an anteater, or more likely from bats, and then jumped to humans. Or perhaps it emerged from a laboratory accident. Or was purposely released from a Chinese scientific facility (insert Asian villain music here). Either way, the new virus proved highly contagious and capable of spreading without any contact, just proximity, through invisible airborne droplets. So this starts off the way any good horror movie should, with a plague rolling in like an invisible killer fog.

Rather than stock market crashes and natural disasters, perhaps the more apt equivalent would be living in Manhattan during my twenties, when HIV/AIDS stalked the population. There was a sudden fear of others, of becoming sick with something for which the mode of transmission was murky and there was no cure, and more than just falling ill, it often meant dying way before one's time. When little was known about how HIV/AIDS was contracted or how to treat it, every time I felt feverish or tired I worried, "This is the end!"

Covid-19 is said to be more contagious and twenty times deadlier than seasonal flu. In order to stay safe, we were directed to stop hugging, kissing, and shaking hands, and to instead bump elbows or tap feet. We were told to wash our hands for as long as it takes to sing "Happy Birthday," and not sneeze or cough near anyone. Still, the dreaded virus snaked its way around the globe, landing hard in the state of Washington, and then New York City became the epicenter, swiftly amassing more cases and deaths than anywhere else in the world. People familiar with the Chinese expression, "May you live in interesting times," were suddenly keen to live in *less* interesting times.

The problem remained that thousands of international flights had been arriving at New York airports for weeks since the virus had devastated China, and as we used to say back home in Buffalo, the horse had left the barn, the cat was out of the bag, too little too late, the ship had sailed, and perhaps most relevant—Mother Nature always bats last.

Being Americans, we immediately sprung into action by purchasing every roll of toilet paper for sale in stores and online, or pilfering it from work or church or the bowling alley. This was despite the fact that most toilet paper is manufactured in the United States, and there was no shortage, and no history of a shortage. Next, we stopped drinking Corona beer, which is imported from Mexico, despite the coronavirus originating in the Wuhan province of China. One could only imagine what might happen to real estate in Corona, Queens.

What's natural is the microbe.

—ALBERT CAMUS,

Chapter 3

Welcome to The Hot Zone

~ꝋꝋ~

When the pandemic began its westward march, I was in Vero Beach, Florida. And having grown up in blizzard-prone Buffalo, I was all too familiar with building a pantry in the certainty that we'd be housebound for several weeks each winter. I rushed to the local Publix supermarket only to find that it was empty, not of products but of people. I was able to buy a warehouse full of hand sanitizer, Clorox wipes, latex gloves, dry goods, canned food, and, yes, miles of toilet paper. When I asked my Fox News–watching neighbors why no one else was shopping, they scoffed and asserted that the coronavirus was a "hoax" being perpetrated by liberal media. "Sign me up, Buttercup," as Grandma liked to say. The one neighbor who did believe a virus might be on the way was stockpiling guns and ammunition.

My last stop before departing Florida was the Dogs & Cats Forever Animal Sanctuary in Fort Pierce. A friend was undergoing a rough winter—she and her spouse split up, her older daughter was having health problems, and her younger daughter, a 4H member, experienced a sheep tragedy. They adored animals and really needed a win, but lived in Albany, New York, where adoptable dogs are few and far between, even without a pandemic. It's best to adopt canines in the South whenever possible since there's a larger number of strays in warmer climates. After making my way past a tub of delightful but yippy Chihuahua pups, I discovered a nine-month-old Australian Shepherd–Dachshund mix perhaps mixed with something else. "Rambo" was caramel brown with a single white paw and resembled a wiener dog on stilts. His card said that he'd lived as a stray in an adjacent neighborhood where he was regularly pepper-sprayed by local homeowners. Ergo, an effusive and affectionate Rambo joined the northbound caravan and had the excitement of being sneaked into a South Carolina Marriott Hotel along with my three dogs. We arrived up north just as his new family was preparing to work and do school classes from home. Rambo was renamed Carl and officially became a "pandemic pup."

Meantime, President Trump announced that he wasn't worried about the coronavirus, and that it would disappear "like a miracle." On March 10 he promised that if we just stayed calm it would go away, that it "was really working out," and "a lot of good things are going to happen." On Thursday, March 12, I was scheduled to throw a fundraising party for the Authors Guild that had been planned months in advance. We hadn't been told to stay home. No one had ever experienced a pandemic—the last one was in 1918—thus we didn't have a playbook. The guest of honor was happy to make her address and the catering team was fine to proceed, so we went full speed ahead, damn the microbes. However, by that afternoon, over half the guests had canceled. As a precaution against hosting a Mary Tyler Moore dud party, I'd invited a dozen friends from church. So long as there's a bar and a buffet, you can rely on Unitarian Universalists to show up during a national emergency, and a plague anticipated to kill over two million worldwide was certainly no exception.

Because I was smugly sitting atop my large Publix stockpile of paper products, I didn't ask people to BYOTP. But just for fun I considered carrying a roll of toilet paper tied to my waist, and having guests request the number of sheets they'd require. It did cross my mind that it might be prudent to pat them down on the way out for hidden rolls, but then I reasoned that people over fifty aren't as concerned about toilet paper since we'd had occasion to use catalog pages and even corncobs in the outdoor privies of our youth. Or else we'd been informed of these alternatives by parents and grandparents reminiscing about outhouse hijinks during the Great Depression, which usually ended with a flimsy wooden shed tipped over on some poor cousin who was forced to crawl out through the crap hole.

The evening went from being called an Authors Guild Night to a Pandemic Party to The End Of The World Gala, and finally, The Last Supper. One editor arrived straight from his *New Yorker* magazine office after they'd closed the building following the discovery of a case of Covid-19 in the nearby World Trade Center complex. Another gal lost her job between hors d'oeuvres and dinner as the family she worked for called to say they'd packed up their car and were fleeing to Savannah, Georgia.

Surprisingly, the party ended up being a real rager, especially considering the average age was sixty. The oldest among us, an actress using a cane following a knee operation, suggested we repeat the gathering every Thursday until we were all gone—a wonderfully theatrical suggestion reminiscent of Agatha Christie's play *And Then There Were None.* It would appear that the secret to a great party is for people to know it's the last time they'll be out socializing for a year, and even better, that attendance could result in death.

We did everything adults would do.
What went wrong?
—WILLIAM GOLDING

Chapter 4

Lockdown

Several "stay-at-home" orders were issued in the US, first in San Francisco and then for the entire state of California. No one was even going to try and tell New Yorkers what to do since they are beyond contrary, subversive by nature, and inherent mutineers.

Instead of being "locked down" New Yorkers were asked to "pause." Ordering them to stay inside would be the best way to have them all head out merely to argue with anyone who tried to stop them. Case in point: The Governor of New York State, Andrew Cuomo, and the Mayor of New York City, Bill de Blasio, were openly feuding. One man would hold a press conference to announce a directive, and the other would follow with a press conference to announce the opposite. A favorite topic for public disagreement was whether public schools would be open or closed, and as a result, millions of people didn't know what the heck was going on. A lot of women, especially those with young children, were exasperated by the rule of old white men. And young people were exasperated by adults, never in a million years thinking that they'd be moaning, "I'd rather be in school!" Parents were similarly promising never again to complain about having to go to work.

On March 20 we were warned to avoid *any* size gatherings and just stay home, or "shelter in place," as if a war was happening in the streets directly out front. Following that, we were advised that if someone in the household was sick or at high risk for contracting the dreaded plague, we must avoid them as well and "self-quarantine." In a small apartment this meant living inside a closet or bathroom. We wondered if anyone made large versions of those hamster exercise balls.

Health directives soon changed from bumping elbows to no contact whatsoever, and remaining at least six feet apart from others ("better six feet apart than six feet under"). This happens to be impossible in Manhattan, where scaffolding encases every other block, thereby forcing pedestrians into dark, narrow corridors, brushing elbows, and with no idea how many people are rushing toward them. Grocery store aisles are narrow to begin with and it's barely possible for two carts to pass without colliding on a normal distancing day. It's also impossible to see if anyone is coming around the corner due to large displays of craft beer and sleepy time tea. Restaurant tables are either contiguous or inches apart. Delis have two side-by-side lines, one for the regulars who know what they want and another for the gaping irregulars trying to make sense of it all. "Social distancing" (keeping six feet apart) on packed subways and buses? Fuhgeddaboudit.

Local coffee shops shuttered their doors, posting signs in the window saying, "Temporarily closed but still AWESOME" or "See you on the other side." My husband, the Rhodes Scholar and Starbucks addict, or perhaps the correct order is Starbucks addict and then Rhodes Scholar, who works as a Columbia University professor specializing in business strategy, suggested we travel by car 1,268 miles from Manhattan to Florida since the Starbucks there had a functioning drive-thru.

Grocery stores remained open, though they appeared to have been devastated by locusts. And so while Chinese citizens were taking dance classes in their quarantine dormitories and Italians were singing from their balconies, Manhattanites were throwing fists in supermarkets over the last can of chicken soup. Trader Joe's on the Upper West Side had become *Lord of the Flies*, with shoppers toppling the greeting card rack on their way to scooping up the last organic avocadoes, goat milk brie, soy chorizo, coconut oil, honey walnut shrimp, chocolate lava gnocchi, and Everything but the Bagel Sesame Seasoning Blend. Bread aisles were ransacked, yet there sat boxes and boxes of Matzoh, which has a shelf life of, well, no one knows. Most imperative, it was the last chance to load up on Mallomars, since these comfort cookies were only "in season" from September through March.

Despite tidying expert Marie Kondo having captivated the nation for the past several years with visions of a simplified lifestyle, massive hoarding was unexpectedly back in style. Pyramids of canned beans, peas, and tomatoes, along with stacks of golden boxes containing a year's supply of Mallomars, appeared all around apartments, including behind toilets and atop headboards. Indeed, no matter our political views, New Yorkers don't have enough space to be survivalists.

Liquor stores were deemed "essential" operations along with pharmacies and ice cream trucks. (Florida Governor

Ron DeSantis declared WWE wrestling to be "essential.") However, liquor stores took precautions, some by requiring employees to wear gloves and face masks, and others with new rules for customers. A Manhattan spirits shop posted very specific guidelines on a sign handwritten in red and blue magic marker: COVID-19 IS SOME REAL SHIT! COVER YOUR FUCKING MOUTH! SHUT THE FUCK UP! BUY YOUR SHIT AND LEAVE IMMEDIATELY. ABSOLUTELY NO TITTY OR SOCK MONEY! STAND BACK AT LEAST 6 FEET, PLAYA. STORE CAPACITY LIMITED TO 5 MOTHERFUCKERS AT ONCE. YOU COUGH, YOU DIE. DRINK RESPONSIBLY. In contrast to what Trump had been telling us, one had to respect the scientific knowledge on display here.

Politicians were apparently correct about liquor stores being essential—they experienced record sales. *Forbes* magazine published "13 Easy Cocktails for the Quarantined" to assist those going "stir crazy." No wonder people were complaining their stimulus checks didn't go far enough, not by a long shot. Wine consumption was no longer measured by the glass but by the bottle and box. Concurrently, Alcoholics Anonymous was running online meetings and chat rooms around the globe, and people enjoyed being able to attend with their friends in other states and even countries.

The longest running joke of all had to be that the entire country was going without pants, as your lower half could not be seen on most video calls and conferences— although it wasn't a joke for reporters on respectable news outlets who appeared pants-less because they thought their legs weren't in the shot. Pants were even awarded a new vocabulary term: "Hard pants" included jeans, khakis, dress pants—anything not soft such as sweats or yoga pants—and the new pre-party question became not "What are people wearing?" but rather "Are people wearing hard pants?" On the bright side, a few lower-level reporters rose to national fame, including Will Reeve at ABC News, who insisted he had shorts on. When the Supreme Court made history by holding arguments over the phone, pants were not the problem, but rather an anonymous toilet flush heard round the nation.

I mailed a large box of books and crossword puzzles to my mother, who lives in a retirement community outside of Buffalo. She's a Rust Belt native who survived the blizzard era when we were all characters in a Jack London novel. Actually, a blizzard was worse; typically the power went out so you were stuck in the cold and dark while everything in the freezer needed to be cooked in the fireplace. The residents in Mom's community had been confined to their rooms, and food was left outside their doors several times a week. I sent her a coffeepot that Google described as "easiest to use for seniors," but she couldn't figure that one out, so I sent a Mr. Coffee like the one we had back in the 1980s. However, the new models use a rinseable filter basket rather than the old paper filters. She insisted that I send paper filters and still won't accept the fact that the basket does the job. She reverted to using toilet paper for filters like we did during the penny-pinching days when people fought over sleeping with the dog at night to keep warm. The next day an article appeared in *The New York Times* titled "Cooped Up, but Upbeat." It did not describe my mother, who had no appetite for spending her golden years imprisoned.

All elective surgery was canceled, which most people assumed meant no facelifts and nose jobs, alarming in and of itself to New Yorkers—but imagine when we found out this meant *all* surgery aside from jump-starting hearts and reattaching limbs. There'd be no cancer operations, gall bladder removals, or splenectomies. Similarly, routine doctor and dentist appointments were postponed indefinitely. My doctor's office closed since it was in a residential building that did not welcome coronavirus-carrying patients showing up for treatment. Meantime, no one dared go near an emergency room. When passing a hospital people crossed to the other side of the street just to be safe. Heart attacks, brain tumors, chemotherapy, and giving birth would all have to wait. Patient, heal thyself. In due course, my dentist sent an email about "telemedicine." I assumed this meant you linked up via computer, threw back a shot of brandy, removed your tooth with a pliers, and then received a bill.

For from within, out of the heart of men,
proceed evil thoughts, adulteries, fornications, murders.
—MARK 7:21

Chapter 5

March Madness

H ave you ever noticed that most disaster films begin
with some of the main characters ignoring science?
One sensed there was a group a people who no longer
believed in anything that they couldn't shoot with a gun.

Jerry Falwell Jr., a close Trump ally, appeared on the TV
show *Fox & Friends* to offer an astonishing explanation for
a plague stalking the land. The President of Liberty University, one of the nation's largest Christian Colleges, suggested
that the North Koreans and Chinese had colluded to spread
the coronavirus inside the United States. "You remember
the North Korean leader promised a Christmas present for
America?" Mr. Falwell asked the hosts. "Could it be they
got together with China and this is that present? I don't
know. But it really is something strange going on here."

It wasn't the first time Jerry Falwell Jr., son of famous
televangelist Jerry Falwell Sr., had dipped his toe into
politics. At a 2015 Liberty University convocation, he

proclaimed the San Bernardino, California, shooting that year wouldn't have occurred if more people had concealed-carry permits to "end those Muslims before they walked in." In 2016, Falwell appeared ready to endorse Texas Senator Ted Cruz for president, and then pivoted to Trump at the last minute. It raised eyebrows that Falwell found the thrice-married, insult-hurling real estate developer with a long history of infidelity and propensity for cavorting with porn stars to be the better candidate. Evangelical Christians have typically sided with politicians who exhibit "family values" and "moral character." Then it came to light that Trump's former fixer Michael Cohen supposedly bought and buried compromising and "kinky" photographs of the Falwells before the endorsement. In true tabloid fashion, the situation involved the couple's sexual arrangement with a pool boy at the Fontainebleau Hotel in Miami Beach.

Jerry Falwell Jr.'s next step was to invite Liberty University students back to its Lynchburg campus following spring break, despite emergency declarations by Virginia Governor Ralph Northam. Keeping the school open would prevent Falwell from having to refund thousands of dollars in tuition fees and boarding costs. However, students and staff began testing positive for Covid-19, as did members of the local community. Falwell continued to rant that closing universities was an overreaction driven by a desire to harm President Trump, while insisting that the media was at its peak of power hunger and authoritarianism since Nazi Germany. Many of the resultant lawsuits are still in progress.

A more convincing theory—to this crowd—about the coronavirus was just around the corner, because it's only a matter of time before any plague is blamed on "the gays." America "is experiencing the consequential wrath of God," Ralph Drollinger wrote on March 21, 2020. Reverend Drollinger led a weekly Bible study group for that bastion of anti-science known as the Trump Administration, and in a blog post titled "Is God Judging America Today?" appeared to blame the coronavirus pandemic on several groups, including those who have "a proclivity toward lesbianism and homosexuality." Drollinger, whom *The New York Times* referred to as the Trump Cabinet's "shadow diplomat," also placed the blame on people with "depraved minds"—environmentalists and those who deny the existence of God—for igniting "God's wrath." The retired professional basketball player and Bible teacher thereby gave an assist to Trump and his evangelical flock as they transitioned from being the pro-life party to the pro-death party.

Meanwhile, friends of mine in Palermo, Sicily, who were already living under government lockdown, pinned their hopes on patron Saint Rosalia to rid the island of coronavirus since she'd purportedly rescued the city from a deadly plague in 1625. Saint Rosalia, a young Sicilian hermit who'd died five hundred years earlier, suddenly appeared and told a resident that if the people of Palermo walked in procession while carrying her relics (to be found in the grotto on Monte Pellegrino), the "evil fever" would disappear. So they were working the pandemic from the exorcism angle.

In New York we were frantically searching for more hospital beds. Central Park is a block from my apartment and its creation was the result of an effort to combat epidemics that regularly swept through New York City in the 19th century. Only now in the 21st century, a sixty-eight-bed tent hospital was being erected in the East Meadow by the nonprofit Samaritan's Purse, which was led by the homophobic and anti-Muslim preacher Franklin Graham.

To work at the evangelical Christian organization, it was necessary to sign a "statement of faith" which included the premise that marriage is between one man and one woman.

Not surprisingly, this Pray Away the Gay operation was not welcomed with open arms in the city of the Stonewall Uprising and where Judy Garland's Carnegie Hall concert moved the entire audience to an altar call. Protesters arrived and local performance artist Billy Talen was arrested for planting a rainbow flag at the site. Two weeks after the hospital opened, God delivered fifty-five mph winds and it appeared the macabre carnival might blow away, like Dorothy in *The Wizard of Oz*, since He works in mysterious ways. However, only the canopy over a staff tent was lost. Next the group attempted to turn the Cathedral of St. John the Divine into an overflow hospital for Covid-19 patients, but was turned down by Episcopalian leaders, who have a history of progressive activism. The church's iconography includes an altarpiece by Keith Haring, a female Christ, jazz great Duke Ellington's piano, and sculptures of Gandhi, Martin Luther King Jr., and Unitarian suffragette Susan B. Anthony.

The sound of concerts and softball games in Central Park was replaced with the shriek of sirens and flashing lights. Instead of lost scrunchies and balled tissues, the bridle path was littered with latex gloves and face masks. SUVs packed with families from the suburbs pulled up in front of my building and hung out the windows while masked grandparents sat in chairs on the curb and had visits. Who ever thought it'd be legal to put on a mask and gloves and go up to a bank teller and ask for money? Or that "I wouldn't touch you with a ten-foot pole" would become government policy.

Videos began circulating instructing people how to properly open packages, which seemed akin to what a bomb squad does. Most tutorials naturally assumed that you had a spacious kitchen, two-car garage, and a backyard, which most New Yorkers do not. Three minutes into the lengthy and involved demonstration on wiping down groceries, I decided there was a case to be made to go lie down on a crowded subway platform and contract coronavirus—just get it over with. I grew up in a neighborhood of large families, and when a child came down with mumps, measles, or chicken pox, mothers corralled them together in a room, oftentimes the same bed. She wasn't going to run an infirmary four separate times—one and done. Those overworked mothers were big believers in not only herd immunity but herd bathing and herd punishment.

Two weeks of high alert felt like more than enough, but the carnage was only beginning. The city's hospitals were overwhelmed to the point where there were gurneys in gift shops, chapels, and conference rooms. Coronavirus was sweeping through sports teams, nursing homes, police stations, fire departments, and Navy ships. Prisoners were four times more likely to contract the virus than the general population. Manhattan was losing transit workers and grocery store clerks and paramedics to the virus at an alarming rate. The news featured shocking pictures of trenches being dug for mass graves in Iran. We gasped, but just three weeks later we were shocked when drones captured footage of mass graves being dug on New York City's Hart Island to serve as the final resting place for hundreds of unclaimed Covid-19 victims. Photos appeared of bodies being stored in vacant hospital rooms and refrigerated trucks were used to hold the dead after some morgues overflowed.

Cuomo took a public swipe at the Brooklyn-born Senate Minority Leader Chuck Schumer in one of his now famous nationally televised press conferences: "It would be nice if he passed a piece of legislation that actually helped the State of New York." Healthcare workers from around the country answered New York's desperate plea to come and help—bless all those who did. Additionally, doctors and nurses were graduated early or asked to come out of retirement. My mother, a retired nurse, received a request to return to active duty. At age eighty-three what did they want her to do exactly? I suggested she could be in charge of helping with crossword puzzle clues.

New York City, the densest metropolis in the United States, had become the area hardest hit by coronavirus on the entire planet. The inescapable fact was that "coastal elites" were being slammed a hundred times harder than the rest of the country. If two months earlier there'd been a movie featuring a deadly virus that attacked only liberals, especially in media capitals, and right before an election, people would've said that's the dumbest idea ever. However, the Poli-Sci-Fi genre was suddenly cinema verité. It was said that Jared Kushner gave a presentation in the Republican White House suggesting that if the virus was killing mostly Democratic voters, then just let it rip.

April is the cruellest month
—T. S. Eliot

Chapter 6

Helter Shelter

While the Democratic party urged people to remain inside, the Undemocratic Party reveled in spring break, indoor weddings, birthday parties, and church services. However, for those who enjoy irony, The Council on Foreign Relations canceled a Coronavirus Conference because of coronavirus.

During the first half of April, the New York metro area recorded an average of over 1,000 deaths per day. It was hard to get tested and the tests were notoriously unreliable. They were also unpleasant—not a spit sample or finger prick but a harsh nasal swab best described as a brain biopsy. Places like South Korea, who had their first victim the same day as the United States, were testing citizens at a much faster rate, and sold five hundred thousand testing kits to America. However, these turned out to be flawed and were never used. Seeing as how South Korea managed to keep their death rate so low (less than one percent of ours), I assume they kept the good tests for themselves.

Wealthy and well-connected people didn't seem to have a problem being tested, along with certain politicians and sports teams, even if they weren't showing symptoms. Many posted their results on the Internet, leaving the rest of us who *were* experiencing symptoms, like me and my husband, to wonder how and why. A joke went around that the best way to determine whether you had coronavirus was to cough into the face of a celebrity.

It was no longer necessary to warn New Yorkers to stay home. With friends and family members becoming sick or dying, combined with the pictures of hospitals under siege and their heroic, beleaguered workers struggling to cope and not fall ill, no sane person wished to ever leave the house again. The days felt similar to 9/11, with email notifications titled "sad news" announcing the demise of relatives, friends, colleagues, and parishioners. As horrible as 9/11 was, it had brought people—even complete strangers—together. When World War II ended, folks flocked into the streets to embrace their neighbors and in some cases complete strangers. There's the famous Times Square photo of a sailor smooching a dental assistant on the lips on August 14, 1945 to celebrate the victory over Japan. In this day and age, there are of course issues with randomly kissing people unknown to you, but we can at least say our serviceman was without prejudice. According to photographer Alfred Eisenstaedt, "I saw a sailor running along the street grabbing any and every girl in sight. Whether she was a grandmother, stout, thin, old, didn't make a difference." Coronavirus ripped people apart. Everything communal was suddenly gone, from sports, brunches, and bars to offices, concerts, and hugs. In the time of Covid we were forced to run the other direction from any and every stranger in sight.

Not even spouses and children were allowed inside of hospitals or nursing homes. People had to say goodbye over iPads, though many victims were already on ventilators and sedated. Plenty of hospital staff, especially nurses, were losing their lives, as well as those working in nursing homes, food banks, grocery stores, and soup kitchens. Before coronavirus, 1.2 million people in New York City were classified as food insecure. The government had no system in place to meet the existing need plus the overflow, which was made even worse with public schools closed.

Manhattan emptied out except for those with nowhere else to go. *The New York Times* "Travel Section" was changed to "At Home." Museums, theaters, shops, salons, gyms, restaurants, and churches were all shuttered. Until then the city always had too much to do. Every evening you were faced with dozens of terrific choices—plays, ballets, movies, comedy shows, lectures, parties, dinners with friends. And these weren't just the options of the wealthy. Local entertainment had always ranged from expensive box seats at the opera to free concerts in the park, from a hot Broadway musical to eating hotdogs in front of a public fountain. Prepandemic, there were street performers in every park and plaza if you included people histrionically fighting on their cell phones. We'd suddenly switched from Fear of Missing Out (FOMO) to Fear of Going Out (FOGO). The city that never sleeps went to sleep. Advertisements for Caribbean cruises were replaced by commercials for indoor gardening. Otherwise, every company switched to basically the same ad—against a background of somber music they insisted your favorite brand was sticking with you and we'd get through these "challenging" or "uncertain" times "together."

A common refrain during this new bizarro world was that we were all in the same boat. However, we were not. We were in the same tempest, but very different boats— from rafts and rowboats to yachts and speedboats. Some would make it to shore and some would not. Some could quarantine with little inconvenience while others faced enormous hardship. Some would watch their stock portfolios rise while others saw their paychecks run out. Some would have everything they needed delivered while others would go out to work and become ill, and in the worst cases, die at home or alone in a hospital room.

Vacation enclaves such as the Hamptons received an onslaught of virus-carrying city folk arriving off season. Grocery stores on the East End of Long Island were not yet stocked with kale chips and Beyond Burgers for the hordes of summer visitors, nor were the small, local hospitals ready for an overload of patients suffering from more than the usual surfing mishaps and sunburn. Several friends considered moving to New Zealand, where they seemed to be handling the pandemic and every other recent crisis with ease, plus there was terrific ziplining. Meantime, the city was getting an influx of new residents as convicts were released from local lockups, especially Rikers Island, since prisons were prime virus breeding grounds not just for inmates but also guards and staff. What could possibly go wrong? (Cars started being stolen at a rapid rate while shootings and street feuds escalated.)

Local New York City restaurants offered takeout, but we questioned whether by ordering from them we were accessories to murder or helping to save livelihoods. The food definitely arrived quickly. There was rampant speeding for the first time in New York City. The West Side Highway became a drag strip complete with mufflers back-firing and neighbors leaping out of bed at 3 a.m. thinking they were being bombed, while first responders had more important things to do. You could drive from the Battery to the Bronx in less time than it took to get there on an express subway train. The number of deadly car crashes skyrocketed. Motorcycle fatalities hit their highest number in three decades. However, speed demons weren't the only lawbreakers; city kids climbed fences to access locked parks and playgrounds. In the leafy suburbs, white-shoed guerrilla golfers snuck onto closed links for nine or eighteen or thirty-six or seventy-two illicit holes.

In our personal lives, standards were dropping by the hour, especially when it came to hygiene. My husband, who had been an executive at Unilever, announced the company was losing money during the pandemic. That's *impossible*, said I, who had been a trader on Wall Street. They sold soap and cleansers and wipes—they should've been creaming it. As usual, the caffeine-swilling professor was correct; Unilever wasn't profiting because people were no longer showering, using deodorant, shaving, or washing their hair with any regularity. That said, I, like many others, washed my hands (including *between* my fingers) more in those months than I had in the past ten years. Makeup also languished in the cabinet. I found out one meeting was dial-in instead of video and was furious that I'd applied lipstick. The next day I put on lipstick before heading out shopping only to remember that I had to wear a face mask—another total waste. About the best one could do was apply some mascara and shadow to get a nightclub-ready smoky eye; but combined with a white face mask and black baseball cap (covering a hundred bad hair days in a row), this only resulted in my looking like a racoon.

The sad truth was that the more we stayed at home, the less we looked like we had homes. Dry cleaners received nothing to clean since everyone was in their pajamas for months on end. There was no need for twenty-four-hour, one-week, or even one-month dry cleaning. Hair and nail salons were dark. People discovered hair colors that had been meticulously concealed for decades, and a lot of blondes just disappeared, though it wasn't from Covid-19. Home hairstyles became known as Corona Cuts. Dogs in Central Park, who'd been the victims of DIY grooming, either looked like they had mange or were part of a punk rock band called Canine-19.

It can indeed be a good thing to have grown up during tough times on a tight budget. There is an entire skill set that includes fixing toilets, changing bed linens, cooking, cleaning, sewing, gardening, sharpening scissors with tinfoil, cutting hair, window washing, bike repair, and furniture assembly, all waiting to be brought back into play. My previous careers likewise came in handy, including dog groomer, camp counselor, short-order cook, cater-waiter, teacher, and stock trader. Unfortunately, tech expert wasn't included on my résumé, because in the recession-battered Buffalo of my youth we were slaves to only three gadgets—the electric can opener, the toaster oven, and the digital clock radio.

A big discovery for many of us who should have purchased hearing aids a decade ago was that wearing face masks made it impossible to piece together sentences through our usual combination of listening, lip reading, and facial expressions. Working at the stock exchange had been akin to being at a rock concert five days a week for years and resulted in major hearing loss. Only on the trading floor I wasn't alone in my partial deafness, and because we all knew sign language in order to communicate over the hullabaloo, hearing loss wasn't really a drawback. However, I now realized how much I'd been cheating by relying on people's expressions along with the movement of their mouths, even though I'd never actually studied lip reading. Surely, it was finally time for hearing aids. The only problem was that I'd have to make them myself with twist ties, flashlight batteries, and whatever else I had around the house.

All of humanity's problems stem from man's
inability to sit quietly in a room alone.
—Blaise Pascal

Chapter 7

Suspended Animation

When Trump was first elected president, we built a new vocabulary that included "emoluments clause," "gerrymander," "25th Amendment," "covfefe," "malignant narcissism," and "people are saying." We quickly added a new coronavirus vernacular that contained some geography, civics, and acronyms: Wuhan, flatten the curve, community spread, super-spreader, silent-spreader, protean enemy, contact tracing, low oxygenation, quarantine bubble, forced innovation, comorbidity, The Swedish Model, Law of Regression, PPE (personal protective equipment), PPP (paycheck protection program), PUI (patient under investigation), Rt (transmission rate), Article 10 (of the Constitution), and, of course, social distancing. People glued to the news learned the name of every state governor plus the definition of "fomite" (rhymes with "toe-blight" and is an object such as a dish or doorknob that may be contaminated). "Travel shaming" would morph from being an indictment on harming the environment to disdain for those who were needlessly spreading contagion. However, my favorite new word was "zoonosis"—a disease that can make the leap from animal to human.

Overnight, we all became armchair epidemiologists who could explain how coronaviruses are a group of viruses affecting humans and animals by causing respiratory illness. In Covid-19, CO stands for "corona," VI for "virus," and D for disease. The 19 was from the year it was first identified—2019. Being a new form of coronavirus, it was often referred to as the "novel coronavirus," which is not to be confused with a newly released medical thriller. In *Sesame Street* terms, if coronavirus was the cat family then Covid-19 was a lion. Meantime, "epidemic" versus "pandemic" made for a good dinner table argument (possibly with yourself).

As life came to a standstill people continuously exclaimed, "Who could imagine anything like this ever happening?" Well, it turns out that computer whiz Bill Gates had predicted the whole contagion mess and explained it all in a 2015 Ted Talk while rocking a bright pink sweater. We'd completely ignored the warning, much to our detriment, since he'd clarified exactly how unprepared we were for such a calamity. Conspiracy theorists were quick to find a more sinister connection and determined that Bill Gates had obviously unleashed the plague. On the bright side, with billions of people suddenly locked inside, the Nostradamus of contagion now had our full attention. Books with subtle names such as *Pandemic* also found a captive audience.

A growing concern for everyone newly working at home, along with first responders and hospital staff who were sent food by appreciative locals, was gaining the "Covid ten" or the "quarantine fifteen." Every day was Taco Tuesday or Pizza Friday. Those who began the pandemic with a surplus twenty pounds or more panicked as experts reported that overweight people were joining the heavenly choir twice as fast as their slimmer counterparts. Most writers and others with experience working at home were accustomed to spending their days a few feet from the refrigerator and the liquor cabinet. As a result, they'd either worked through those relationships, or in the case of several colorful author friends, they had not. The main problem with being a writer during a pandemic, particularly a novelist or humorist, is that it quickly became impossible to compete with reality.

For those addicted to late-night doomscrolling (another new entry to our corona vocabularies), there was no shortage of scary headlines:

"Could Children Be Super-Spreaders?"

"How the World Missed the Silent Spreaders"

"52 Who Worked or Voted in Wisconsin Election have Covid-19"

"Global Deaths Top 300,00 with No Evidence of Immunity"

"Tennessee Restaurants Reopen as State Sees Biggest 1-Day Jump in COVID-19 Cases"

"These 9 Hand Sanitizers May Contain A Potentially Fatal Ingredient"

"Why Picking Your Nose Is Dangerous in the Time of COVID"

"Llamas Hold Key to Conquering Covid-19"

"Coyotes on the Prowl"

"CDC Warns Aggressive Rodents Are Looking for New Food Sources"

"Rabbits Are Facing a Deadly Virus of Their Own"

"Seven More Big Cats Test Positive for Coronavirus at Bronx Zoo"

"First Dog Infected with Coronavirus Has Died"

"Scientists Studying if Dogs Can Sniff Out Covid-19"

"Death-Cap Mushrooms are Spreading Across North America"

"Just Because You Test Positive for Antibodies Doesn't Mean You Have Them"

"Doctor Gets Coronavirus Through Eyes"

"Can Mosquitoes Spread Covid?"

"Plants Get Sick Too"

"Could Doomsday Bunkers Become the New Normal?"

"Have You Considered the Benefits of Crying?"

Even scarier, these are all from reputable sources and mostly, if not entirely, true. And that's why "Doctor Says Coronavirus Could Be Spreading Through Farts" is not on the list; despite the amount of serious discussion it received, the claim appeared to be false.

The unanswered questions kept coming. Why were five times as many older people dying as younger people? (A trend that millennials, who blamed the senior citizens running things for this mess, cynically termed "boomer removal.") Why were men dying at a much higher rate than women? The president and his three remaining challengers were over seventy years of age and the front-runners were male. With masks, social distancing, and working from home, people wondered if this was the end of the #MeToo movement.

While it was the finest hour for many Americans who continuously risked their lives to serve others, inevitably there were scammers. As the virus lodged in people's lungs, baloney lodged in people's brains. One had to be wary of offers for home testing kits in exchange for payments or personal information. Televangelist Jim Bakker (who'd stepped down from *The PTL Club* after a sex scandal and spent several years in prison) was sued by the state of Missouri after hawking "Silver Solution" for $80 a bottle, which was not only ineffective when it came to preventing coronavirus, but could actually be dangerous to your health. Texas radio host Alex Jones was ordered to stop selling toothpaste which he insisted "kills the whole SARS-CORONA family at point-blank range." Toxic hand sanitizer was for sale. Phony charities sprung up, along with fake offers of toilet paper.

Crackpot conspiracy theorists swore that coronavirus was caused by 5G transmitters, which persuaded arsonists in Britain to attack more than ninety cell towers. Rumors that Covid-19 could be cured with cocaine gained so much traction in France that the government was forced to make an official statement to the contrary. The governor of Nairobi, Kenya, while outfitted in sunglasses, mask, cap, and shield, proclaimed cognac as a "throat sanitizer" that "kills the virus." Drinking methanol, another mythical cure, led to more than seven hundred deaths in Iran. A Japanese religious group called Happy Science that trafficked in lost continents, UFOs, and demonic warfare was now selling "spiritual vaccines." A video called *Plandemic* insisted that a shadowy cabal of elites were using the outbreak and a possible vaccine to gain power and make money. Meanwhile, Donald Trump was hawking the untested hydroxychloroquine as a miracle cure, which would turn out not only to be ineffective against coronavirus, but also to have potentially adverse side effects, including death. However, that only caused Trump to double down and claim that he was in fact taking the drug himself.

As for entertainment, it felt as if the entire nation was watching the true crime documentary series *Tiger King: Murder, Mayhem and Madness* the same way we'd all watched *Roots* during the Blizzard of '77 in Buffalo. Those binging on travel videos were said to be taking a "coronacation." My Kindle sent me an unsolicited message announcing that I'd been reading a lot lately. No kidding. Every newspaper and magazine contained stories about past pandemics, assuming that during a horribly depressing lockdown nothing could be more fascinating than reading about previous epic plagues that devastated millions. When it came to television, I'd been wanting to watch the British detective series *Inspector Morse* for decades, and with thirty-three episodes almost two hours apiece, I decided that it should keep me busy enough.

People spent more time with their pets, and animal shelters around the country were overwhelmed by those fervently wishing to become pet parents. Back when I'd picked up Rambo (now Carl) in Florida, I had no idea what a smart investment that was and should've taken a dozen homeless animals. Shelter websites changed from featuring adorable photos to announcements that they were cleaned out—even Dolly the opinionated twelve-year-old dachshund with "chronic medical issues" who "doesn't get along with other dogs and cats or children" managed to find a forever home. Next there was a run on bicycles, swing sets, trampolines, cabins in the woods, Oreo cookies, and Grape-Nuts cereal. (The Grape-Nuts nuts didn't seem concerned that the cereal contains neither grapes nor nuts.) This was followed by a shortage of nickels and dimes—finally some "Breaking News" that not a single person in New York City cared about.

Easter Sunday church services were streamed online. However, the New York Governor's daily briefing popped up during my church's sermon and I shamelessly switched over to Andrew Cuomo. Apologies to Jesus, but with over 7,000 New Yorkers dead and local hospitals past the breaking point, I was more interested in the resurrection of the city and life everlasting in my neighborhood.

Kids had most of their lives canceled, including sports, activities, lessons, parties, and playdates, so the six-year-old moppet down the hall was at loose ends. She loves my dogs, so we spent hours playing in the corridor with balls, bones, empty boxes, and balloons. The dogs, both male and female, had their hair styled and nails painted every color of the rainbow. We built forts, played Pickle in the Middle with the rambunctious Frenchie, and had foot races. There were ferocious games of Uno, Old Maid, Go Fish, Dominoes, Chinese Checkers, and Jenga. Uno required an entire day of study on my part, largely because the moppet alters the rules depending on her mood and the state of play. Twister necessitated a warm-up at my age. Clicking the plastic dome covering the Pop-O-Matic Trouble dice drove the Frenchie berserk, so he could be counted on to end that game prematurely by snatching the board between his teeth and running away with it. I hadn't played the Game of Life in forty-five years. It was an updated version with action cards that took into account the modern world. When I landed on the opportunity to marry, the moppet handed me a blue peg husband. It appeared a good teaching moment and I remarked that I could also marry a woman and take a pink peg. The moppet proceeded to marry a cat, so clearly she didn't need any tutorials when it came to freethinking.

Endless, uninterrupted hours of playing that didn't involve video games or computers was a whimsical return to my 1970s childhood. However, whereas I'd found the Game of Life exciting as a ten-year-old—contemplating all the choices and excitement that lay ahead—at age fifty-five it was rather dispiriting that the game *ends* where I am in real life. How about an update with retirement choices including whether to volunteer, select a hobby, or take a low-paying job because interest rates are practically zero and your savings are earning nothing, or else babysit the grandchildren because your own kids (who are living with you and working two jobs) can't afford the expense of childcare?

Some days we were thrown all the way back to the 1950s. My church began a Zoom group for knitting and crocheting. Parents took kids through the car wash for excitement. Board games such as Monopoly, Parcheesi, and Clue appeared in family rooms across the country. The only difference was that you could Google the rules rather than try and read the small print inside the box top. With regard to the detective game of Clue, the real mystery was, "What happened to Mrs. White?" (The matronly housekeeper was killed off in a 2016 feminist coup.)

They're coming to get you.

—

Chapter 8

Wild Kingdom

⌒⟲⌒

Fifty thousand people were dead from coronavirus nationwide and the great unraveling continued. Amid the economic slowdown, the price of oil tanked, and on April 22, a roll of toilet paper was officially worth more than a barrel of oil. Nevertheless, we didn't care that oil was basically free, because when it came to mileage, we were all getting ten weeks to the gallon (if your car hadn't been stolen). Later that day, Senate Leader Mitch McConnell proclaimed that blue states with lots of coronavirus should declare bankruptcy rather than be funded by the federal government in order to continue running their hospitals, schools, sanitation, and police departments.

The following morning there was a freak hailstorm. Next, White House advisor and right-wing economist Stephen Moore proposed giving everyone a spacesuit so that businesses could reopen. Nurses were protesting in front of hospitals because they didn't have enough protective equipment, but everyone would get a spacesuit—on what planet? Still, the day wasn't over. By nightfall we were half-expecting to be hit by a meteor, but instead, President Snake Oil Salesman went on national television and suggested injecting disinfectant or ultraviolet light into your body to kill the coronavirus. This caused the makers of Lysol to put out an official statement saying that under **no circumstances** should their products be administered into the human body, as if partying teenagers had been in the news for chewing Tide Pods before throwing back Jell-O shots.

The country was so sidetracked that no one paid much attention when "murder hornets" arrived on our shores the following week. They'd traveled across the Pacific from Japan and first appeared in Washington State (why not DC?). These Asian giant hornets come armed with long stingers and venom lethal enough to kill a human being, although their favorite pastime is decapitating bees. The invasion was quickly followed by another in a series of crap-your-pants headlines: "Murder Hornets Aren't the Bugs You Should Worry About." (It's mosquitos because they carry illnesses that kill more than 700,000 a year.)

However, it was more than just bugs bugging us. Emptied-out Main Streets around the world were now host to all varieties of new window-shoppers including wolves, alligators, warthogs, wild goats, hippos, monkeys, coyotes, pumas, kangaroos, bears, otters, ostriches, and even penguins! Plus a few I had to Google, including civets, javelinas, capybaras, and Nubian ibexes. A family of foxes took up residence under the busy boardwalk in Toronto's Beach neighborhood. Sea lions and turtles reclaimed shorelines while kangaroos and iguanas assumed control of more than one golf course. A man in India drove around a corner on his motorbike only to find that "oncoming traffic" was an elephant. A tetchy bald eagle attacked a $950 government drone above Lake Michigan and sent it hurtling to a watery grave following a brief aerial battle. So much for being the national bird.

In New York City, a three-foot eastern rat snake slithered along a Brooklyn subway platform, possibly in search of Pizza Rat. One New York City councilman remarked that the snake moved faster than the R train. The Metropolitan Transit Authority, whose motto is "If you see something, say something," could not track down the interloper and requested riders to immediately report any suspicious reptiles. A story ran in *The New York Times* titled "Is That You, Yogi? Here's Help in Telling One Bear from Another." Was this a skill that would soon be required on the Upper East Side of Manhattan? In Washington, DC, reporters outside the White House were being hassled by raccoons while trying to film their news segments. Who needed zoos? In fact, we were the ones now confined to our cages to be gazed at by the animals. It was becoming clearer by the day that nature was fully prepared to take over the minute we were out of the way.

Who was that masked man?

—FROM

Chapter 9

Pandemics for Beginners

I belong to a small minority of Americans who grew up wearing a face mask. During the long Buffalo winters a bank robber–style, over-the-head woolen mask protected one from vicious blizzards and made skiing possible in subarctic temperatures. However, it wasn't long ago that New York City had one of the highest murder rates in the nation, and no one wanted to be reminded of the bad old days. Anyone who'd survived the crime-ridden New York City of the 1970s or 80s had an entirely different association with people wearing masks and were reminded of risking their lives just to enter the subway or walk through Central Park in broad daylight. Venturing out during the pandemic became reminiscent of that calculation—was leaving home worth risking death? Only back then it was a guy with a gun, and now it was a fatal disease.

New Yorkers celebrate Halloween with more gusto than any other city with the world's largest parade, and still residents aren't partial to masks. Furthermore, traditional hospital masks are not fashionable. There's no way to dress them up or down or make them a part of any ensemble whether your look is legal eagle, tech whiz, skate rat, hip hop, cool dad, or lady who lunches. Plus, when coronavirus broke out, medical workers were desperate for masks, and community-minded civilians didn't wish to be seen taking one away from a health care professional.

With New York medical facilities overwhelmed and no sign of the Federal Government hospital ship on the horizon, it felt like Civil War times. Just as women had repurposed linens for bandages during the bloody battles of the 1860s, Governor Andrew Cuomo put out a call for citizens who could sew masks. There were YouTube videos on how to make them at home. And on April 1 *The New York Times* print edition carried a full-size pattern with mask-making instructions that took up an entire page, titled in large letters HOW TO SEW A FACE MASK. But it wasn't an April Fool's joke.

However, my name isn't Betsy Ross, and I couldn't sew for my country because I hadn't paid any attention during home economics class back in 1978. It was the final days of mandatory cooking and sewing classes in public school, and we gals joked our way through learning to can preserves and hem skirts as we prepared to become doctors, lawyers, journalists, and engineers. I was instructed to make an apron and brought it home so my mother could sew it for me. Still, even Mom would toss her push pedal Singer sewing machine to the curb and become a nurse in 1980, and shortly thereafter I left for Wall Street. My junior high school discarded its ovens and replaced them with science laboratories.

To address the mask shortage, I logged onto Etsy.com but all that came up was an informational letter about

Covid-19. In the bottom of my scarf drawer was a stack of bandanas left over from my summers as a camp counselor. Once every year I'd almost toss them out since they just sat there taking up space. But something always held me back because in the olden days a bandana could save your life by serving as a tourniquet after snapping a limb or being bitten by a rattlesnake. So now I had masks, and by placing a coffee filter between the folded fabric, they were almost medical grade. Still, I looked so much like a bank robber that the doormen made guns using their thumb and index finger and shot me every time I walked through the lobby. Finally, all the creative designers who'd been furloughed from Broadway and the fashion world started making masks featuring skulls, subway maps, and Yankees emblems that complimented every look and New Yorkers could wear with panache.

In mid-April Governor Cuomo issued an executive order that all New Yorkers must wear masks when going outside if not able to socially distance. There'd be no arrests or tickets because he decreed there'd be self-policing, i.e., if you were on a street corner not wearing a mask the person next to you would ask, "Hey Buddy, where's your mask?" Any New Yorker who has ever witnessed a confrontation over not cleaning up after a dog or smoking a cigar in a public park knows that self-policing is indeed a popular New York sport (that occasionally ends in death). However, "self-policing" means "SELF-policing." And when Mayor Bill de Blasio encouraged New Yorkers to rat out rule-breakers by sending photos of the offenders to a government agency, the tip line was immediately flooded with dick pics.

I've been residing in NYC since 1983 (the year Trump Tower opened), and it was the first time I ever saw the subways clean. As with any crisis, coronavirus hit the poor harder, and subway fare evaders could be seen donning gloves and spraying turnstiles before leaping over them. Social distancing continued to be mathematically impossible on an island of 1.6 million that is thirteen miles long and two miles wide—especially when most of the residents were not going to work or school. People crammed into small apartments count on the fact that family members or roommates will be out for up to eighteen hours per day. Competing for sidewalk space were strollers, dog walkers, workers replenishing store inventory after massive hording, and hundreds of delivery people. Lobbies, elevators, and mailrooms were often less than six feet by six feet to begin with. Construction continued, go figure. There'd never be a break from the deafening sound of jackhammers in Manhattan, not even during a pandemic. Most contractors received special dispensation by insisting that roof work was being done, and the structures would be compromised if left unfinished. Much like everyone's dog was supposedly an emotional support animal, everyone was now in need of roof work.

Central Park was the new Grand Central Station. The Black Hawk choppers that had been noisily flying overhead at low altitudes since 9/11 were suddenly and blissfully absent. However, weddings from all over the city had been relocated to the Park at the last minute, complete with musicians, caterers, and long dresses dragging across the damp ground. Another few thousand residents were attempting to get some exercise after their gyms, pools, yoga studios, tennis courts, and Soul Cycle shops had closed. Many were clearly escaping families and roommates, while others were coordinating to meet friends and loved ones. Boomboxes had been set up and dance parties were underway. The only thing missing was a disco ball and Donna Summer's "Hot Stuff." It was one large microbial cloud, like my trading pit on Wall Street during a particularly vicious outbreak of pink eye, or the time my entire elementary school was visited by chicken pox. I won't name Patient Zero in the chicken pox fiasco, since he stills feels bad about it five decades down the track, but in truth we can all be thankful for a lifetime of immunity.

Spring arrived and allergies hit hard. With climate change it seemed that every year we encountered new forms of plant life invading from the north or south that aggravated our nasal passages. It was impossible to tell if you were sick with Covid-19 or felt wheezy from walking through freshly mown grass or a haze of tree pollen. Either way, it necessitated digging into our precious reserves of paper products.

Senior citizens who, only a month ago could barely operate a self-serve gas pump or ATM, suddenly became rampant computer users. People hosted Zoom cocktail parties and drank Quarantinis. Homebound workers threw "Zoom shirts" over the backs of chairs to quickly slip on before a meeting and many kept a Zoom lipstick nearby. There was intentional "Zoom bombing" by children and roommates, and unintentional Zoom bombing by toddlers, pets, grandparents, and naked spouses. A church meditation group was Zoom bombed by Nazi porn, whatever that is. I hope they regained their center.

Early on there was the woman who brought her computer to the bathroom during a meeting. A dutiful husband could be seen taking out the trash in the background. Participants regularly shouted I'M MUTED when they were NOT MUTED. There were newscasters and entertainers trying hard to get their dogs into the shot, but needed to bribe them with treats. There was the lawyer who appeared as a large-eyed kitten in virtual Zoom court and informed the judge, "I am not a cat." Several months in, when it was assumed most office types had figured out the basics, Senator Tom Carper of Delaware yelled, "fuck, fuck, fuck" on live television during congressional testimony as he got up to speed on how to use videoconferencing. And CNN legal correspondent Jeffrey Toobin probably thought *fuck, fuck, fuck* upon losing his job at the *New Yorker* magazine following "an incident"— Toobin was under the impression his colleagues couldn't see him during an election simulation Zoom meeting while he engaged in erection stimulation.

Zoom was now employed for school, work, therapy sessions, volunteer planning, banking, shopping, book groups, concerts, singalongs, exercise classes, astrology readings, job interviews, board meetings, church services, Bingo games, astrology readings, museum visits, home buying, theater, parties, and adoption. Even James Joyce's Bloomsday—an occasion for celebrating *Ulysses*—became a virtual Zoomsday. Whereas "Zooming" had until recently been a verb, it now meant the complete opposite of racing from place to place. Even the dating scene moved to Zoom. Articles appeared touting "phone sex is safe sex," and romantic activity on video became known as a "Zooty Call." One heading proclaimed "Boundaries Can Be Sexy," as if returning to the Victorian era was a good thing.

A Twitter account called Room Rater that allowed ranking quarantine quarters of celebrities and newscasters as viewed online became an overnight sensation. Al Roker landed an enviable ten out of ten on a call with Business Insider, while presidential candidate Beto O'Rourke received a zero in an interview with the Cambridge Union Society (but the interview got a good review), and one observer called for an "organize rescue mission" to aid O'Rourke. Meantime, the United Nations Security

Council received a collective two out of ten, which is abysmal when you consider all the spectacular flags they have for set design. Queen Elizabeth II received a perfect ten for her April 5 address to the nation—and that was *without* corgis, hat, and handbag, but of course she rocked a brooch and pearls.

The Internet jokes were flying. A picture of a couple disembarking from a cruise ship with dark tan lines where they'd worn surgical masks went viral. Revised NCAA brackets had Purell battling OxiClean, and Clorox pitted against Softscrub. There were videos of public health officials holding serious press conferences instructing the populace not to touch their faces while the presenters were touching their faces. My favorite photo was of a United Kingdom verdant vigilante who dressed up as shrubbery to escape lockdown orders.

Fake announcements filled the e-waves:

The US Government is taking the coronavirus seriously. I hear that new testing methods are being done without even leaving your house! No hospital or office visit necessary! All you have to do is mail a stool sample to:

Donald J. Trump
1600 Pennsylvania Ave.
Washington, DC

Donald Trump, our toddler king, announced that he took no responsibility for the pandemic spreading like wildfire throughout the US nor for our overall unpreparedness, but he had absolute authority when it came to reopening the government. Ruling America was a giant ribbon-cutting ceremony to him. Only you couldn't force most New Yorkers out of our homes for the occasion. That said, when it was announced that Starbucks in China had reopened, I thought for sure my husband would have us on the next flight to Beijing.

It is sometimes an appropriate response
to reality to go insane.
—Philip K. Dick

Chapter 10

War on Covid

———— ❧ ————

While riding the elevator in my building a woman announced that she was going to kill her husband and save Covid-19 the trouble. I didn't think for a moment that she was joking. Bottom line: No one wanted to spend this much time with ANYONE. Similarly, all the singles were frustrated that it was impossible to go out in search of a mate. The main argument happening was who in lockdown had it worse—marrieds or singles—until a spike in alcoholism proved it was actually those quarantined at home with young children.

Meanwhile, we found out who the puzzle people were—some had been embedded within families for decades without anyone knowing. Others experienced "quarantine envy" of those with beach houses, inground pools, finished basements, and Peloton bikes. A careful study of online photos caused a flurry of rumors about who had managed to sneak in some plastic surgery.

Friends who sold real estate were worried about short-term sales, but encouraged by all the divorces and teen emancipations caused by close quarters. There was talk of a Coronavirus Baby Boom from those who'd made the best of being confined, which would send growing families in search of more space. I was familiar with the latter, or at least a Blizzard Baby Boom. In elementary school the teacher would ask everyone's birthday during the first week of school by calling out the month and requesting a show of hands. Eighty percent of the class was born in September or October, including me.

On April 3, 2020, New York state reached a truly miserable milestone. Over the course of nearly five weeks, the coronavirus had taken 2,935 New York State residents, which was more than the 2,700 killed on September 11, 2001 when terrorists flew airplanes into the World Trade Center. The disease had claimed moms, dads, grandparents, siblings, and even children. The death toll was only expected to grow, and grow. But perhaps the cruelest turn of fate was that a number of pals who had miraculously survived 9/11 were killed by Covid-19.

By this time most of us had been sick or knew people who were sick. Sick with what, who knew? My husband and I felt like we had several flus at once with weeks of sinus aftermath. Testing was still not widely available, especially if you weren't a celebrity or working in the White House. If you braved the trip to a medical facility for a test and didn't have Covid-19, there was a good chance you'd have it by the time you returned home. Meantime, more than half the tests were still showing false negatives. This was the corona conundrum. But even if we hadn't been sick, the virus remained very real to us. We all knew at least one person who'd died by now, but for most the number was considerably higher. Yes, many of the victims weren't young, but they weren't done either, and in most cases, we assumed they had another good decade or so ahead.

Some people became very ill and others not at all. Many experienced in-between levels of sickness and oddly lost their sense of taste and smell. Surfaces were suddenly touted as not being as deadly as previously thought, while gathering outside appeared to spread fewer infections than inside. Ventilators, once thought to be the secret to surviving bad cases of coronavirus, were now viewed as a death knell. In mid-April it was announced that people with type A blood were at significantly higher risk for contracting the disease and those with type O had the least risk. One wondered if there was any news on the impact of eating coriander or knishes; it was beginning to seem like absolutely anyone could hang out a shingle and claim to be an expert on the disease by saying the first thing that popped into his or her head, much like the president did.

Working from home now had its own acronym— WFH. If the downside was shrieking children, barking dogs, and camera-blocking cat butts, the upside was no commuting, having windows that opened, and access to a thermostat. Experts began raising issues such as "The Sanity Index" and "Quarantine Fatigue." InfoWars' Alex Jones threatened to eat his own neighbors if the lockdown continued. Rates for addiction, mental duress, domestic violence, apocalypse anxiety, and time-share remorse were on the rise. Anti-shutdown protesters were arming themselves and gathering at state capitols in various parts of the country, even on May 2, when the national death rate from Covid-19 hit an all-time high, and the number of Americans infected crossed the one million mark (along with a million comparisons to equivalent numbers killed in wars).

The White House coronavirus response coordinator Dr. Deborah Birx, aka The Scarf Lady, announced that precautions were still needed at "protests against precautions." Seriously. You'd be forgiven for thinking it was part of a comedy routine. Especially since Vice President Mike Pence was visiting the Mayo Clinic and then a nursing home without wearing a mask, contrary to the policies of his own Task Force, and President Trump was at a mask factory, of all places, not wearing a mask. Mishandling a pandemic received its own new word: pandemicide.

Governor Cuomo, our new collective Dad, took a harder line, shouting at New York protesters during a nationally televised press conference: "Wear a mask, not a chin guard. It is the law." He demonstrated the right way to wear a mask (covering your face) and the wrong way (covering just your chin while leaving nose and mouth exposed)—"This is nothing. I don't know what this is. This is like a form of a chin guard. That's what this is. It may be a fashion statement. It may be cool. But this accomplishes nothing. It's not a mask. It's nothing." Talk about an optimist, the man was trying to potty train an entire country that appeared delighted to run wild in crappy nappies. Meantime, people who wore their masks incorrectly became known as "maskholes."

Two days later it was revealed that a White House military aide, one who brought the President his meals, had tested positive for coronavirus, along with multiple members of the Secret Service. The following day it was a top aide to Mike Pence who tested positive for the virus. Trump reacted by visiting nonagenarian World War II veterans that same afternoon without wearing a mask. "Is Trump Trying to Spread Covid-19?" Tom Friedman asked in his *New York Times* column.

Manhattanites, who are known for their rowdy natures, and had been isolated longer than the rest of the country, in more confined spaces, were *not* storming City Hall. They were saying "thank you" like an updated version of *Goodnight Moon*. Thank you door persons, thank you delivery persons, thank you transit workers, thank you hospital workers, thank you grocery store clerks and pharmacy workers and postal employees. To avoid putting their families at risk, many of these people had spent several months living in their workplaces, basements, cars, garages, RVs, backyard tents, and even kids' treehouses. Thousands of medical professionals had voluntarily traveled from relatively Covid-free parts of the country to help, and stayed in rental apartments, dormitories, and hotels. The Italian tradition of singing to pandemic heroes transferred to New York City, but unable to come to a consensus around a single musical genre, residents leaned out windows or stood on rooftops and balconies cheering, ringing bells, and banging pots and pans.

Mankind, you are yourself to blame.

—Goya

Chapter 11

Apocalyptic Spring

⌒⟿⌒

O n the heels of the plague and murder hornets, a record-shattering polar vortex arrived on Mother's Day weekend. The May storm pummeled an already pandemic-battered Northeast with wet snow, below freezing temperatures, and wind gusts of over forty mph. For most cities it was colder than it had been on Christmas Day. In addition to "stay-at-home" orders a "freeze watch" went into effect. The historic storm brought with it a biblical sense of finality to our existence, even for Unitarian Universalists. We could only hope that it was the darkness before the dawn. However, that afternoon Governor Andrew Cuomo issued an executive order extending New York's State of Emergency until June 6.

In mid-May, manufacturing workers and those construction workers who'd been sent home were allowed to return to work if they followed certain rules, most involving masks and social distancing. Also, stores were permitted to take your order and bring the merchandise outside, which was dubbed "curbside retail" and added a whole new meaning to a "drive-by" in New York City.

Cases of coronavirus in New York State were finally declining, although outbreaks were rising in other parts of the country. On the subject of spikes, the temperature in Manhattan shot up to eighty-four degrees on Friday, May 15. It was an important date—the one originally listed as the beginning of the end of our long confinement. However, only five regions in New York State were allowed to begin reopening, while NYC was put on lockdown for *another* month. Hey, whatever happened to giving us the bad news gradually, like when teenagers wreck the car and try to soften you up first by saying, "No one was hurt."

"Blursday" became shorthand for no longer knowing what day of the week, or even month, it was. People no longer described things that exponentially gained in popularity as "going viral," while "being positive" was similarly burdened with an ominous new meaning, and "pass the corona" stopped being a party starter. The pandemic had been ravaging the country for six months. What else could possibly go wrong? Dams broke in Michigan, causing a state hard-hit by Covid-19 to suffer massive flooding. It wasn't surprising that people were wondering only half-jokingly, "Where are the locusts?" As it turned out, the locust invasion was in India, along with steadily increasing coronavirus, a massive heat wave, and a killer cyclone. Meanwhile, the Eastern United States was invaded by millions of seventeen-year-cicadas, and the deafening buzzing noise sent many residents of North Carolina, Virginia, and West Virginia right back inside their homes for another week, while a few fled to underground bunkers. I suppose it'd be an ironic twist if there were any more ironic twists, but we appeared to be in a death spiral of irony.

Though absent a buzzing noise, it became apparent that coronavirus was causing more than its fair share of devastation in the commercial world. We all become amateur economists, conversant in "monetizing the debt," "the V-Curve," "the U-turnaround," and "FAANG stocks." Retailers such as Neiman Marcus, JCPenney, Pier 1, Papyrus, Aldo, Roots USA, GNC, True Religion and Modell's Sporting Goods threw in the towel. Hundreds of local mom and pop shops called it quits, while thousands of restaurants closed their doors for good.

There was also bad news on my pandemic viewing of *Inspector Morse*. Spoiler alert (but the series is over thirty years old): the inspector's girlfriend leaves him and he dies at the end. Whoa! In any crime series the bad guy perishes while the good guy gets the girl and his dream life, or at least the chance to continue inspecting things. Where was the good news? Amazon founder Jeff Bezos became the world's wealthiest person, so that was clearly good for him. The rest of us had to settle for fewer school shootings, not as many pedestrian deaths, and shorter commutes. And women felt there might be a win for them in the fact that female world leaders were managing the pandemic best while their male counterparts were bungling it the worst.

On May 27 the first space shuttle to launch in nine years was postponed due to thunderstorms. I've never had much interest in being an astronaut or even flying in planes, but suddenly space sounded appealing. Of course there'd have to be two-day shipping.

Laundry is the only thing that
should be separated by color.
—Anonymous

Chapter 12

Minnesota Burning

———~oͽo~———

Just when I thought this long, strange trip was coming to an end, society collapsed.

The hellfire and brimstone came from an unexpected place on Monday, May 25, and the goalposts were once again forever changed as to what a "new normal" might look like. The Twin Cities erupted in demonstrations, burning, and looting when a video surfaced of a white Minneapolis policeman executing a black man by keeping his knee on the man's neck even after he was subdued and in handcuffs. Three more officers were in attendance as George Floyd called out, "Please, please. I can't breathe," and then died while bystanders begged, shouted, cursed, and recorded the killing on cell phones. The four white officers were fired from the police force, but two and a half days later still hadn't been taken into custody or charged for the murder of forty-six-year-old George Floyd. Derek Chauvin, the officer who killed the unarmed Floyd, had at least seventeen prior complaints against him on file with the Minneapolis Police Department's Internal Affairs Division. The same day as George Floyd's death, a white woman was captured on video in Central Park calling the police on a black man she claimed was threatening her. In fact, he was birdwatching and had simply asked her to leash her dog in an area where signs clearly stated that dogs should be leashed. This launched the term "Karen" into widespread use, which denoted white women using their privilege at the expense of others.

George Floyd's murder was a tipping point after four hundred years of institutional racism, complicated by a pandemic that was hitting communities of color at least twice as hard and revealing a host of underlying social ills. Cases of coronavirus were spiking in Minneapolis and ICU beds were full. The following day police officer Derek Chauvin was taken into custody and charged with third-degree murder and second-degree manslaughter. Yet Floyd's family and the protesters deemed this too lenient and wanted a charge of first-degree murder. Furthermore, the other three officers who'd been at the scene, and considered accessories to the murder by many, were still in the comfort of their own homes. Demonstrators wished to see all four men prosecuted and properly sentenced, which they well knew rarely happened in police brutality cases.

In addition to becoming overnight stay-at-home epidemiologists, we now were amateur criminologists. Once again there was a new vocabulary to master, which included "excited delirium," "excessive force," "chokehold," "spit hood," "Antifa," "Boogaloo Bois," "Black Wall Street," "pepper balls," "MAGA Night," "Proud Boys," "qualified immunity," "no-knock warrant" and "dominate the battlespace." The small percentage of violent police officers were "bad apples," and the small percentage of violent protesters were "bad actors." We'd also be learning the difference between "murder" and "manslaughter" along with the varying degrees of each. (Manslaughter is an unlawful killing that doesn't involve malice aforethought, but often the line isn't clear.) Fortunately, the *Perry Mason* TV series was being revived on HBO.

People began taking to the streets. That was certainly one way to end a lockdown during a pandemic. Most protesters wore masks, but there were thousands, and they weren't exactly socially distanced. Concurrently, many police officers didn't wear masks despite the pleadings of New York's Mayor and Governor (the one thing they agreed upon?). I suppose the good news was that if we didn't already have "herd immunity," we just might in a few weeks' time.

The SpaceX rocket finally launched from Cape Canaveral on May 30, but it was slightly overshadowed by the disintegration of the country. Cities were issued curfews, including Minneapolis, Seattle, Portland, Denver, Atlanta, Los Angeles, Cleveland, Columbus, Pittsburgh, and Philadelphia. As for the places where the general populace was already in lockdown, it sounded counterintuitive. Once again, Governor Andrew Cuomo knew his New Yorkers—despite the lockdown still in place, he didn't tell people to stay home; he just begged people to wear masks when out protesting, like a parent urging teenagers to dress warmly in winter. Because if you tell New Yorkers they can't do something, they will do it, even if they didn't want to do it beforehand and don't really want to do it now. New Yorkers are oppositional, opinionated, resistant, and subversive, because those characteristics help them survive and even thrive in a place where a million other people are trying to do the same things at the same times every day. It so happened that Andrew M. Cuomo was from Queens, which was also where Donald J. Trump grew up.

On the night of May 30, protests erupted in cities from coast to coast despite at least forty curfews and the National Guard being summoned to many places. In short order, America was burning. Government buildings were set alight, windows were shattered, stores were ransacked, monuments were vandalized, firecrackers were exploded, and bricks, rocks, and water bottles were thrown while authorities in riot gear launched rubber bullets, tear gas, pepper balls, flash-bang grenades, and smoke bombs at protesters. Police also employed Mace, tasers, batons, and stun guns. The White House finally went into lockdown mode.

In New York City, demonstrators in all five boroughs scuffled with police, blocked traffic, marched, and a crowd paused at Trump Tower in Manhattan. Police cars were burned and hundreds of protesters were arrested. Outside of the Barclays Center in Brooklyn, officers and protesters "traded projectiles," as *The New York Times* delicately put it, and many bystanders filmed aggressive and disturbing behavior by demonstrators and police alike. In *The Crucible*, Giles Corey says "more weight" as he's crushed to death with heavy stones. It appeared we needed "more film"—basically a recording of every police encounter from start to finish. Having split the atom, put men on the moon, and cured polio, this doesn't feel like a tall order. In fact, my local ATM manages this 24/7. Studies show that when attendants are proffering towels near the basins in restrooms, handwashing suddenly triples.

Initially, I thought the only thing the pandemic had in common with the 1960s was that many women stopped wearing bras. But overnight we'd gone into full Civil Rights mode. However, the rioters of the 1960s had been largely people of color raging against an unfair justice, education, and economic system. Since then, enormous disparities in wealth had resulted in enormous disparities in political influence, and thus policies, no surprise. For instance, the minimum wage, adjusted for inflation, remained lower than it was in the 1960s. And white officers still policed predominantly black neighborhoods miles away from where they lived and sent their own children to school.

Trump's MAGA slogan was a problem in and of itself. When you proclaim, "Make America Great Again," what time period exactly is being referenced? Evidently one in which large groups of people were disenfranchised and actively discriminated against, including but not limited to women of every color, Native Americans, Blacks, Hispanics, Jews, Muslims, atheists, people of various sexual orientations, and those with disabilities.

This time round there were people of all colors and faiths raging against an unjust system and the presidency of Donald Trump, who was clearly not overburdened with a social conscience. Seeing a five-foot-one white female elementary school teacher carrying a sign reading, WHITE SILENCE = WHITE VIOLENCE! and a gay couple holding hands chanting, "Say his name!" was a stark contrast to the lineup of mostly Blacks versus mostly whites in the 1960s. Not only that, but some police officers were taking a knee in solidarity with protesters. This uprising felt unique in how multigenerational, multiracial, and multisexual it was, along with how it was not just happening in big cities, but also small (predominantly white) towns. Unlike previous demonstrations, there was also an alarming number of people in mismatched military gear with no identification on it.

Late one afternoon I was packing meals at my Unitarian Universalist church soup kitchen when we received a "riot alert." This is clearly different from being read the "riot act," but no less alarming. The church is on the Upper East Side and not all that far from Gracie Mansion, the mayor's residence, which was going to be an assembly point. Since it's the Upper East Side, I asked if the memo had any instructions regarding how to dress. Nobody laughed. I strolled through the protest on my way home and it was fairly peaceful. But after days of news stories unpacking the reasons for the unrest, and what it was demonstrators hoped to accomplish, I couldn't help feeling like the whole world had suddenly converted to Unitarian Universalism. For my entire life we'd been hammering away at antiracism, social injustice, and inequality, week after week, with sermons, lectures, protests, petitions, and Sunday School classes where we sang "This Liberal Light of Mine," but for decades it was as if we'd been living in a tiny bubble—what folks called "a fart in a windstorm" when I was growing up in Western New York. As a kid there were so many times I couldn't go with friends to see a movie on the weekend because we had to march for the United Farm Workers, RID (a precursor to MADD), NOW, ERA, AIM, NARAL, gay rights, or against the Vietnam War. (This was despite my grievances about child labor violations after many hours were spent making protest signs in a church basement.) All the people whose books we'd studied and lectures we'd attended were suddenly on every channel; it felt as if we were having a giant coming out party that had been a long time in coming.

Having grown up in a time and place of urban unrest, I was familiar with this story. I was born into fire—during the assassinations of Malcolm X, Rev. Martin Luther King Jr., and Robert F. Kennedy; race riots; abortion battles; bra burnings; and Vietnam protests. While my friends

were rocking out to Kool & The Gang, I knew all the
words to Phil Ochs's "Draft Dodger Rag," including:

> *Sarge, I'm only eighteen, I got a ruptured spleen*
> *And I always carry a purse*
> *I got eyes like a bat*
> *And my feet are flat*
> *And my asthma's getting worse*

Living in Buffalo, it was always hard to decide if the
world would end in fire or ice. Despite some epic blizzards,
the fire people, in particular the Catholics, appeared to be
in the lead. They always did have the numbers, costumes,
and enthusiasm.

Growing up, my father was a court reporter and my
mother was a nurse in the inner city. My uncle was a police
reporter and we were well aware that being an officer of
the law is a dangerous job. Still, at the age of eight I also
knew that a "throw down gun" was an untraceable weapon
dropped at a crime scene to justify a bad shooting. Similarly, I was aware that many problems stemmed from
manufacturing having moved overseas, and the systematic
ghettoization of communities where economic and social
challenges ran deep. The result was poor living conditions,
bad education, exploitation, violence, lack of opportunity,
and mass incarceration. We learned that from watching our
cities burn in the 1960s, yet a half century later, very little
had changed. And the nearby Seneca Nation of Indians
(their word), suffered from a similar narrative, but it was
even more deeply concealed from the general public.

Historically, pandemics have forced humans to break with the past and imagine their world anew. This one is no different. It is a portal, a gateway between one world and the next. We can choose to walk through it, dragging the carcasses of our prejudice and hatred, our avarice, our data banks and dead ideas, our dead rivers and smoky skies behind us. Or we can walk through lightly, with little luggage, ready to imagine another world. And ready to fight for it.

— ARUNDHATI ROY

Chapter 13

Uncivil War

President Trump claimed that his supporters were coming to protect the White House (they didn't), that anyone moving on the White House would be met with "the most vicious dogs and the most ominous weapons," and retweeted "The only good Democrat is a dead Democrat." It's just a guess that the protests had morphed into a referendum on the entire Trump presidency. Live footage played on every news channel and photos appeared on the cover of every paper while the Tangerine Spleen tweeted FAKE NEWS.

Talk about being whipsawed—just as we were finishing our canned goods and frozen foods, it was time to restock. The culture wars had moved from shouting on cable news to battling in the streets. I suppose it shouldn't have come as a surprise. When Trump had addressed uniformed police officers three summers earlier, he disparaged those who cradled the heads of suspects as they tucked them into squad cars and proclaimed himself an admirer of rough "justice"—"You can take the hand away, okay?" A bank of officers seated behind him laughed and cheered. The President continued, "I have to tell you, you know, the laws are so horrendously stacked against us, because for years and years, they've been made to protect the criminal. Totally made to protect the criminal. Not the officers. You do something wrong, you're in more jeopardy than they are."

Protesters in Toronto, Berlin, and throughout the United Kingdom marched in solidarity against police violence. One could draw a parallel between Donald Trump's Right Wing and Boris Johnson's Brexiters. By the sixth night, there were demonstrations in every state with no end in sight. It may have been a school night, but there was no more school. Furthermore, the pandemic had left many people unemployed or still working from home. Theaters, sports arenas, bars, restaurants, and nightclubs were still closed. You had to go to Georgia to get a tattoo. We'd caught up on all our favorite shows and no new episodes could be filmed, so it wasn't like the entire country had anywhere else to be.

More curfews and states of emergency were declared, but as darkness fell, vandalism, arson, and violent encounters between police and protesters once again inflamed the nation. All this in the midst of a virus that continued to rage, with fewer cases in the Northeast but spikes and hotspots throughout the rest of the country. Our new schedule was: go outside and bang pots and pans to thank essential workers at 7 p.m., have dinner, then head out with placards and water bottles to protest at 9 p.m. There was little time to change from Covid clothes to riot ensembles. In addition to our new face masks and latex gloves, we now needed helmets and shields to venture out. On the bright side, a mask doubled as a barrier against tear gas, pepper spray, and smoke bombs. In just a few short weeks a mask had become a don't-leave-home-without-it multipurpose garment. The bigger the better.

For three long months Trump had desperately tried to steer the conversation from the thousands of Americans dying of coronavirus. Only this was a perfect déjà vu storm. Three major crises of the past century—Spanish Flu of 1918, The Great Depression of the 1930s, and the Civil Unrest of the 1960s—all managed to repeat themselves in a single moment. Many retail businesses that were already hanging on by a thread suffered damage, looting, and burning. Customers who were just beginning to emerge from their cocoons returned to hibernation to pull up the drawbridge again. It felt like feudalism, barter, and droit du seigneur were just around the corner.

The only thing left was for Trump, who loved nothing more than playing arsonist–fireman, to come out from hiding in his underground White House bunker to fan the flames. Like clockwork, the President of the United States called state leaders "weak" and urged the nation's governors to use force and "dominate" the protesters to take back the streets.

The tripping point occurred on Monday, June 1, 2020. Peaceful demonstrators were forcefully removed from a park near the White House before curfew so Trump could facilitate a photo-op in front of a church he didn't attend holding up a Bible he didn't read. Police and the US military drove away demonstrators using smoke canisters, tear gas, pepper balls, rubber bullets, flash-bang grenades, horses, and riot shields so Trump could proclaim himself a "law and order" kind of guy. Perhaps most disturbing was the sight of low-swooping Army helicopters creating powerful gusts that sent dirt and debris flying at protesters while drowning out everything else. Anyone over fifty-five was immediately reminded of the fall of Saigon at the end of the Vietnam War. And anyone who has lived near Niagara Falls was well aware of the high accident rates for helicopters.

New York City was issued an 11 p.m.–5 a.m. curfew. It was the first curfew since 1945, when Fiorella LaGuardia was mayor and Franklin D. Roosevelt was president, and only five thousand homes had TV sets. Allied forces had just bombed the city of Dresden in Germany, the United States was facing a shortage of coal and gasoline, and the director of war mobilization ordered a nationwide midnight curfew on all "places of entertainment."

Mothers everywhere know that nothing good ever happens after midnight, and definitely not social justice. Another problematic issue in New York was the open secret that Governor Andrew Cuomo and New York City Mayor Bill de Blasio had a toxic relationship, while de Blasio and the New York City Police Department had an even more poisonous association—so noxious that cops had turned their backs on him at funerals.

The curfew did little to deter vandalism and marauding gangs of looters—in fact, it only seemed to encourage starting the carnage earlier. Macy's flagship store on Herald Square was ransacked along with Nike, Coach, and dozens of neighborhood businesses. Windows were shattered in the SoHo and Flatiron neighborhoods. Graffiti was sprayed across signposts and buildings, including the block-long Squadron A Armory on Madison Avenue on the Upper East Side. Scaffolding was set ablaze and there were at least a half dozen fires in the Bronx.

The next morning our evening curfew was brought down from 11 p.m. to 8 p.m., except for essential workers. The funeral of George Floyd was on June 9, but another disturbing consideration was that the three accomplices to his murder still hadn't been arrested. People who'd hesitated to leave the city for the Covid crisis were quickly rethinking their plans—only good luck finding a rental anywhere within a hundred miles of New York City. The number of people protesting grew but most of the violence was finally quelled.

The 8 p.m. curfew in New York City was extended through the rest of the week. Meantime, Trump was talking smack about Andrew Cuomo and the Governor's younger brother, Chris Cuomo, a newscaster on CNN. Anyone in New York during the 1980s was aware that Mario Cuomo may not have run for president because of rumors about his mafia ties. So Trump went ahead and taunted Chris Cuomo as "Fredo," a fictional character in *The Godfather* who is the doomed family ne'er-do-well. The saddest part of this might be that Trump hadn't even thought up the insult himself. Still, it was a big mistake, and clear to anyone from New York that the Cuomos would end Trump. When the brothers responded in the press that day, they may as well have given the President *il bacio della morte* (the kiss of death).

Emperor Trump had promised a "beautiful" wall at the Southern Border (paid for by Mexico), and now a very ugly wall went up around the White House, turning it into a fortress. This Trump "rally" wasn't in a stadium with devoted followers but had him cornered inside by a disgruntled mob of voters outside. He was actually forced to cancel a weekend of golf. This was the nation's largest protest movement in a generation and showed no signs of letting up. Corporations were making statements and commitments. Even the NFL came out and said they'd been wrong about discouraging those who knelt on one knee at games to protest police brutality. However, I didn't see the NFL offering a job to Colin Kaepernick, who'd begun the symbolic gesture and lost his livelihood over the backlash.

Finally, we all had toilet paper, but the FDA announced a shortage of the antidepressant Zoloft and its generic equivalents. Day twelve of the protests brought a record crowd to Washington, DC, while demonstrations continued across the country and around the world. People wanted not just accountability, but actual change. It was over fifty years since Martin Luther King Jr. and Malcolm X had been assassinated while fighting against systemic racism, and yet here we were. There was a call for sweeping reforms that included outlawing chokeholds, a stop to the militarization of local police, more transparency of police officers' records, better training, more police living where they served, independent investigations into wrongdoing with fewer delays, limiting immunity, and diverting a portion of the police budget to address community challenges. There was a call for more control over the powerful unions that fought recommended reforms and oversight.

The American Revolution may have begun with "the shot heard round the world," but a pattern of abusive practices had been building up for years. Likewise, the current situation. Underlying all of this was chronic voter suppression and a system that gave each state, no matter how populated, two Senators, so the minority was ruling the majority. Meantime, the pandemic had exposed racial inequalities in a harsh light, and so had the devastation and depression-level unemployment left in its wake. For instance, "essential workers" were in large part low-paid grocery cashiers, shelf stockers, warehouse workers, delivery people, home health aides, and municipal employees.

There needed to be more equity in education along with better housing and health care.

It certainly helped the prevailing mood when the charges against Derek Chauvin, the officer who'd knelt on George Floyd's neck, were elevated to second-degree murder. And finally, the other three officers at the scene were being charged with aiding and abetting murder. Protests continued, but on balance became more peaceful.

And what is so rare as a day in June?
Then, if ever, come perfect days...
—JAMES RUSSELL LOWELL

Chapter 14

Discovering the New World

Despite high rates of the virus in half the states, all had reopened partially or completely by June 1. The death toll in the New York City metro area was declining, along with the number of new cases and hospitalizations. However, a thousand Americans were still dying from coronavirus every day.

The local curfew was off; then it was on; then it was extended; then it was enforced; then it was ignored; and then it was suddenly called off altogether. Like everything else this year, you never knew exactly what was happening, and when you thought you had it figured out, it abruptly changed. It may as well have been the 1800s with everyone getting updates via pony express or packet steamer. I was reminded of John Adams losing out on a second term for president because news of the diplomatic peace he'd achieved with France was still on a ship sailing across the Atlantic.

For New Yorkers the "pause" officially ended on Monday, June 7, 2020, one hundred days after the first coronavirus case was confirmed, and after eighty long days of lockdown at the epicenter of the worldwide outbreak. More than 210,000 New Yorkers had been infected and at least 22,000 had died. In its darkest time the city was losing a resident every other minute. Practically a *million* jobs had been lost, there was a 9-*billion*-dollar shortfall in the budget, and 52 percent of young adults (18–29) were living with their parents, the most since the Great Depression.

We were exhausted by worry, fear, anxiety, Zoom squares, televised press conferences, "Breaking News," board games, DIY anything/everything, food delivery, family, beards, and baking bread (sourdough was the most popular—should we be reading something into that?). And most of all, we were sick of hearing the words "the new normal." Perhaps the only distraction people hadn't tired of was digital games, based on the steep rise in revenues for those companies. Playing Fortnite and Minecraft had seamlessly replaced living, with a large percentage of the world's population disappearing into a parallel universe online. Who could blame them?

After having been quarantined near the end of winter, we emerged from self-storage at the start of summer, blinking in the sunlight like bears coming out of hibernation. It was a beautiful day—sunny and cloudless, but not too humid. Only due to the recent protests, stores and restaurants were boarded up as if a hurricane was about to hurtle up Madison Avenue. Warnings about masks and social distancing continued from responsible voices. The rate of new infections was down, but far from zero. I was certain I'd had coronavirus, but lacked any proof, since when I felt poorly back in March, tests were few and far between, and largely inaccurate. However, I knew from growing up in blizzard country that one can only endure (or "embrace" if you're a Buddhist) endless games of Monopoly and Uncle Jack's day drinking for so long before you finally say to hell with it, I don't care, and out into the storm you venture, because suddenly it's worth a dance with death to skid across black ice through a whiteout to have a blue raspberry Slurpee.

The city streets filled with cars and trucks and cyclists, playgrounds were overrun by energetic kids, and sidewalks overflowed with pedestrians, baby carriages, and people walking their pandemic pups. For the first time in its history, Manhattan ran out of bicycle parking. The sound of cement mixers replaced the wail of sirens. Nevertheless, it was a new world of protest graffiti, police barricades, face coverings, latex gloves, and plexiglass shields. (Why didn't I invest in plexiglass back in January?) Every restaurant, bank, museum, salon, and store in the state was installing plastic barriers. Entrepreneurial vendors added bandannas, masks, and pocket-sized hand sanitizer to their tables of hats, scarves, and sunglasses.

We checked in on our pants, and most no longer fit. It turned out that if social distancing from others was hard, social distancing from the fridge had been almost impossible. A few people had used their saved commuting time to lose weight, while a friend who'd been hospitalized six weeks with Covid lost an incredible forty pounds. However, those on the mac n' cheese and hot pocket diet had experienced waistline expansion. Fortunately, it was seventy-nine degrees outside and time for shorts.

The lockdown had created such a multiverse of parallel worlds that it was a comfort to reenter the "real" one, or at least the old one. In New York City about twice as many women as men were wearing masks, while about twice as many men were dying of coronavirus. Just an observation.

The United States had officially entered a recession back in February despite the galloping stock market—another emblem of our upside-down sideways world. Wall Street prospered while Main Street suffered, and with interest rates at zero, retirees had no safe place to invest their money for even a low but steady and safe return. Society definitely appeared to be on the brink of collapse. There was talk of investing in cryptocurrencies like Bitcoin and Ethereum and storing them on Blockchain. However, most of us over forty couldn't tell them apart from the digital coin Dogecoin, which had been started as a joke, and Eleuthera, an island in the Bahamas.

Over a million people had been out protesting for two weeks straight and then returning home to family members, roommates, and social circles. But they wouldn't begin to find out for another week, after moving through the incubation period, if they were infected with Covid-19. And if there was a sudden surge in cases, was it from reopening or demonstrating or both? In essence, once again, we were a citywide, nonvoluntary, all-inclusive science experiment. To make things more interesting, the World Health Organization (WHO) put out a statement that confused everyone about whether or not asymptomatic people with Covid-19 could spread the disease.

The next day, as new cases around the globe hit a record high, the WHO changed its mind about asymptomatic transmission being very rare. I doubted I was the only one reminded of Mark Twain's quote, "If you don't like the weather in New England, just wait a few minutes." Managing the disease appeared to be up to us. With regard to contagion, we needed to upgrade our virology education by learning about disease vectors, natural immunities, and the difference between asymptomatic spread and presymptomatic spread and nosocomial infection. Unfortunately, I still don't know the difference between viral and bacterial pneumonia even though I've had both. Otherwise, "nosocomial" sounds like an up-and-coming neighborhood in Northern South Brooklyn, but actually means a disease which originates in a hospital.

It was reported that researchers were in the process of developing more than 125 coronavirus vaccines. A headline the next day asked, "Does Getting Sicker Make You More Immune?" That sounded about right. We'd all have to go back to school for immunization microbiology, study up on the D614G mutation and the "cushion effect," and decide for ourselves. It would be a whole new category of cocktail party chatter, if we ever returned to having parties.

The voice I was hearing in my head on Tuesday, June 9, 2020, was not that of infectious disease doctor Anthony Fauci or presidential hopeful Joe Biden or Al Sharpton (who was eulogizing George Floyd), but Dorothy Parker's "What fresh hell is this?" My beloved hometown of Buffalo was finally making news for something other than blizzards. Renegade Trump tweeted that the seventy-five-year-old protester who'd fallen backward and cracked his head on the pavement after being pushed by police was an "Antifa provocateur" deliberately trying to make law enforcement, and by extension, Trump himself, look bad. Needless to say, the claim was false.

After several weeks the Black Lives Matter protests were still going strong. There was a call for immediate action with regard to items that had been on the political agenda for years, such as rechristening military bases named after Confederates and removing statues and portraits celebrating supporters of racism, some of which had been erected as recently as the late 1970s. However, the demonstrations themselves in many cases had transformed from political events to cultural happenings. Rioting had turned to angry demonstrating to peaceful protesting to what was now more like a rollicking block party with music and lawn chairs and coolers. The energy was still there, and the call for the status quo to go, but the brouhaha had taken on the feeling of street life, and that felt right for such a groundswell. Besides, there certainly weren't any other theaters, concerts, sporting events, or gatherings to attend. Even the malls and gyms were still closed.

By mid-June, cases of Covid-19 were rising in over half the states, and the jury was still out on how much the many demonstrations would further spread the virus. There were already instances of National Guard members and police officers who'd worked at the protests being infected. Then came another classic 2020 headline: "Contact Tracing Is Most Powerful Weapon but As Cases Surge the Proven Strategy Is in Doubt." (Which was already obvious to those of us who use Pennsylvania Station or Central Park.) So now it appeared that thousands of contact tracers had just been hired, trained, and paid for naught, costing several states a small fortune, all of which could have gone toward paying the teachers and nurses they'd soon have to lay off due to massive budget shortfalls.

Lockdown came to an end just as I caught up on my work. However, I'd also vowed to clean out my desk, drawers, closets, and cupboards, but none of that happened during fourteen weeks at home. I once shared a commencement platform with the brilliant economist Lester Thurow, and while we were waiting through a lengthy technical delay in the blazing sun, he recollected how three years of unread magazines and journals had accumulated during a particularly demanding job. Then he had an epiphany—if you wait long enough, you can toss everything without even sorting through it. Not long after that he died, which serves to confirm his theory and add to it—if you wait even longer, you can let someone else worry about it. Thank you, Lester—let's call this the Thurow Doctrine.

In New York City, the first big weekend of the Phase One reopening did *not* go well. Pictures and videos appeared online of large parties with few masks and no social distancing. Revelers gathered six deep in front of bars and restaurants, hanging out on sidewalks, spilling into streets. Andrew Cuomo was *not* happy. Guv Dad held a resoundingly stern press conference to single out groups in Manhattan and the Hamptons, and everyone was threatened with a return to lockdown, having the car keys taken away, being grounded, and a big time-out all around. Mr. Executive Order called the social distancing violations "rampant" and threatened to cut everyone off by revoking the liquor licenses of establishments caught breaking the rules. After tweeting, "Don't make me come down there" he even picked up the phone and personally called proprietors violating the rules. We all felt Guv Dad's anger and disappointment, and either promised to do better or else hide our transgressions with more proficiency. Mayor Bill de Blasio decided to be Mom in this fight over the kids misbehaving and shot back that shutting down the city again wasn't the right answer. Mayor Mom wanted to talk things out and employ more "social distancing ambassadors" for a socially distanced group hug. Guv Dad was having none of it—there'd been a fresh outbreak in Beijing, and after a hard six months of stressful work he was in no mood for more Covid-19.

Then Daft Uncle Donald chimed in with his two cents: "We'd have very few cases if testing stopped." That made perfect sense, like if we did less pregnancy testing there'd be fewer babies.

Life is like a sewer: what you get out of it
depends on what you put into it.

—Tom Lehrer

Chapter 15

Family Feud and Turbulent Toilets

⟶ ∽ ⟵

We were instructed to be "hyperaware" when using the lavatory since a new study showed how "turbulence from a toilet bowl" can create a "large aerosol plume" that may carry coronavirus particles to the next visitor. "Is it Safe to Let People Use Your Bathroom?" blared the headlines.

Like every other gyroscopic day in the time of coronavirus, more kooky-sounding bad news followed a few hours later: Apparently your pets couldn't give you coronavirus (back to my new fave word: zoonosis), but you could give your pets coronavirus! So, if you were ill it was necessary to "socially distance" from your pets inside the home, and from animals on farms and at zoos. The Covid-19 learning curve grew steeper by the minute.

Governors, columnists, and psychologists kept insisting that by following our "inward pilgrimage," we were going to build a *better* world. Indeed, the old one had its drawbacks, especially in New York City—JFK airport comes to mind, as does the R train, and $15 for a glass of wine from a $12 bottle. Still, most of us would have been delighted just to have our flawed world back.

June 17, 2020 was another action-packed day with more threads than a God's eye. Mayor Bill de Blasio said he didn't see New York City being ready to enter Phase Two of the reopening process until early July, and the decision would be made in close cooperation with the state. That was all Governor Cuomo needed to hear to call a press conference and announce that New York City would enter Phase Two on Monday. This meant we could get haircuts by trained professionals! Restaurants were allowed to offer outdoor dining, and in-store retail would begin. For those with Post Traumatic Pandemic Disorder (PTPD), an upstate bed and breakfast was offering cow cuddle therapy sessions for $75 an hour, and they were completely booked.

Meantime, journalists had received advance copies of the new John Bolton book, *The Room Where It Happened*, which the White House was trying to halt through legal action. A series of stories appeared saying that Bolton had the goods to impeach Trump all over again, since the president outright asked China for help getting reelected, which is illegal. Trump also had a habit of granting personal favors to dictators. To distract people from these accusations, the Great Exaggerator announced that the vaccine for AIDS was proof that scientists could develop one for coronavirus. Only there wasn't a vaccine for AIDS.

More conundrums followed. Liberals were sending the new Bolton book around via the Internet to read for free as a political statement. And as an author dependent on royalties, that should worry me. Perpetrators argued that instead of being patriotic and testifying about what he knew, or acting as a whistleblower, Bolton desired only to profit, and in doing so had betrayed his country and let Trump off the hook.

On Saturday, June 20, the Great Exacerbator held a campaign rally in Tulsa, Oklahoma. Coronapalooza was shaping up to be a giant super-spreader event. No masks or social distancing were required, although you had to sign waivers promising not to sue the Prez if you fell ill. Trump's system for vanquishing foes was to give them a nickname and then ferociously deride them; coronavirus was now the Kung Flu, but it wasn't retreating into the shadows. The fact that Covid-19 cases were climbing in several states, including Oklahoma, was merely an inconvenient truth. The virus was no longer being discussed in terms of waves, but rather a forest fire that would burn as long as there was fuel.

Protesters were agitated about Trump's rally, even after it was switched from the day before, Juneteenth (celebrating the anniversary of slaves in Texas receiving news of their freedom in 1865). Many remained outraged that it was taking place near the site of the 1921 massacre in which a white mob slaughtered Black residents and destroyed Black-owned businesses and homes in a community known as Black Wall Street. The Trump campaign was preparing for a million supporters to come pledge their fealty, and even built an outdoor stage for the overflow crowd. But only sixty-two hundred showed up, which is less than 1 percent of the million Trump was expecting. It appeared that Trump had been punked by a bunch of meddling kids, who'd registered for the event online with no plan of attending. The Prevaricator-in-Chief used the opportunity to reiterate that the problem behind increasing coronavirus cases was definitely testing, and he was going to ask for less testing so there'd be fewer cases.

Six members of the Trump advance team tested positive for coronavirus, as did two members of the Secret

Service, and at least one reporter, which was clearly the fault of over-testing. Two days later, two more Trump campaign staff members who'd attended the Tulsa rally tested positive. The following day, Trump headed to Arizona, which was seeing a steep increase in cases and deaths. Residents hadn't been doing much by way of social distancing, and the Republican governor had prevented Democratic mayors in the state from requiring face masks.

Trump held an event in Phoenix at one of the nation's largest megachurches, which claimed to have an air purification system that "kills 99.9 percent of Covid within ten minutes." I could only wonder how the commissioner of basketball, Broadway producers, and the director of the Metropolitan Museum of Art hadn't been able to get their hands on this God-given technology—what idiots! Didn't they want to reopen? Or perhaps the answer was to be found in the name of the Assemblies of God megachurch, which was, and I kid you not, called Dream City.

At the same time, Trump was busy trying to stop publication of *another* tell-all book, this one by his niece Mary Trump, the daughter of the president's late brother Fred Trump. *Too Much and Never Enough: How My Family Created the World's Most Dangerous Man* was touted by its publisher as being "revelatory." Since Mary had a master's degree in literature and a doctorate in psychology, many saw her as the perfect author for such an inside look. Meantime, Trump was accusing former President Barack Obama of "treason" (a crime punishable by death) without offering any evidence.

Insanity is relative. It depends on
who has who locked in what cage.
—RAY BRADBURY

Chapter 16

Going Through A Phase

By the second week of Phase One, contact tracing was not going at all well, to no one's great surprise. The specially trained disease detectives were finding many New Yorkers to be elusive and obdurate. Those who'd been exposed to the virus were supposed to be quarantining and getting tested. Many claimed to be home when they were out and refused testing. A few insisted they had a twin who made a Starbucks run or was spotted drinking outside of a bar. (However, they weren't shy about asking for grocery deliveries.) Instead of people with health care backgrounds, officials should have hired workers who were more dogged, cynical, and persuasive, such as bounty hunters, repo persons, and the folks who chase down student loans.

Nevertheless, Phase Two of reopening began in New York City on June 22. Only now it was harder to get a haircut appointment than it was to get a coronavirus test. Likewise, dinner reservations were nearly impossible as restaurants were operating at much lower capacity while facing months of bottled-up demand. Kids gleefully went on outdoor playdates, much to the relief of parents, nannies, and neighbors. Subway ridership was up to a whopping 17 percent, though still closed between 1 a.m. and 5 a.m., in part for cleaning but also as an organized method for removal of permanent dwellers. Street vendors had really upped their pandemic game and in addition to hand sanitizer and medical face masks, they were now hawking "fashion masks" with designer names and team logos along with colorful prints, cartoons, and animals for children. (Let me clarify that the leopard, tiger, and snakeskin motifs were merely patterns printed on cotton fabric, as opposed to the retailer in Florida who was selling masks crafted from *actual* alligator, crocodile, and Burmese python skins.) Also available were clear plastic face shields, latex gloves, and Brand X wipes. Office workers were permitted to return to their socially distanced elevators, restrooms, and cubicles. However, at the entrance to many buildings the health police took temperatures with a thermometer that looked like a gun aimed directly at your forehead. And dogs had a collective nervous breakdown when we left the house without them.

Still, unlike Phase One, people didn't seem to be in a rush to head back to the office or life in general. I saw numerous moving vans being loaded up while every second business had shuttered for good, and wondered if the city would ever truly recover. People had said New York wouldn't come back after 9/11 but it did, and then some. During the bubonic plague in the 14th century cities were declared to be dead, yet the Renaissance followed.

Directly after New York City entered Phase Two, and continued to report fewer coronavirus patients, hospitalizations, and deaths, the United States overall logged five days of record numbers of new coronavirus cases, and on July 1 a record of over 50,000 new cases was reported in a single day. The next day was over 55,000 and the day after that over 57,000. The solution: Close the bars! (Although that felt counterintuitive since doesn't alcohol kill germs?) The US represents just 4 percent of the world's population but had a quarter of all coronavirus cases. On average, more than 1,000 Americans were dying every day, and 130,000 had already succumbed. Sometimes it's not good to be number one, and this is especially true with regard to Covid-19 deaths. The European Union announced that despite how much they wanted our tourist dollars, until we pulled our epidemiological act together, the US was on their no-fly list along with Russia and Brazil. Make no mistake, the Canadians had no interest in allowing Americans to cross the border either. Not even if we were bringing diapers, Barbies, and Levis, or Diet Cherry Pepsi and Speculoos Cookie Butter from Trader Joe's.

The South and the West began experiencing a surge in cases. Several states were backtracking on their reopenings, including Republican-led Florida and Texas. Meantime, I was hearing a new phrase every few minutes—"(Fill in name of city) is getting like New York." When the virus surged in Los Angeles, they described it as "Our New York Moment." The words "New York," which for two centuries had meant the capital of commerce and culture, now translated to one thing: Hot Zone. It reminded me of growing up in a suburb of Buffalo; after manufacturing pulled out and unemployment skyrocketed, residents began fleeing the inner city. The first ring suburb of Amherst grew so fast that it became a zoning hodgepodge with traffic problems. Still, despite good schools, health care, theaters, restaurants and shopping, "becoming like Amherst" was endlessly used in a negative sense.

Perhaps the only good thing to arise from the coronavirus resurgence in other parts of the country was that mask wearing in New York jumped from 80 percent to 98 percent overnight. Apparently even the "nobody tells me what to do" crowd didn't want to go back to what it had been like in April. However, wearing a mask in the rest of the country had been turned into a political decision despite their proven efficacy in stopping the spread of the virus. Regardless of state directives, many police officers interacting with each other and the public at close range were not wearing masks.

The temperature shot up to 90°F while the humidity was "jungle," and masks were uncomfortable. Internet tutorials popped up explaining how to avoid or treat mask acne or "maskne." Another problem was that we all kept tripping over curbs and our own two feet since masks tend to block one's downward vision. Avoiding dog poop was also an issue since many side streets were sparsely populated and pet owners became positively cavalier about not picking up after their dogs, which confirmed my suspicion that most people only scoop poop because other people are watching. Women who'd been pregnant had an advantage since they'd trained themselves to feel around with their toes or bend over for a better look at potential obstacles.

It was hard to get used to taking a mask when leaving the house and putting one on before getting out of the car to enter a store. Masks now hung from rearview mirrors the way plush fuzzy dice had back in my youth, or a St. Christopher medal if you were Catholic. My biggest challenge was remembering to grab a mask before walking the dogs since I performed the task on autopilot. However, in July I made a wonderful discovery—dog poop bags (with handles) are masks! Granted, they're very hot masks and you will suffocate eventually, but it beat waiting for an elevator (only two people at a time under Covid restrictions) to go back and get one.

For the first time in two months that old aerosol band The Coronavirus Task Force was getting back together for a show, though missing its lead performer, The Disease Vector-in-Chief, who back in late April tweeted that they weren't worth his time anymore. Trump and VP Pence still insisted that the problem was not the virus, but too much testing. Just like cancer patients should blame testing for their tumors. And we could eliminate sexually transmitted diseases if we'd only stop testing for them. The virus had killed 125,000 Americans over a few short months and Trump equated it to "a kid with the sniffles." Pence took it a step further and said to pray away the plague. "Just continue to pray that, by God's grace, every single day, each of us will do our part to heal our land." Trump and much of his cabinet and advisors were now said to have "negative credibility," which is different from "no credibility," in that their remarks weren't just dismissed as baseless, but understood to be most certainly wrong, and the opposite was probably true. Case in point: Pence's *Wall Street Journal* editorial on June 16, 2020, insisting there'd be no coronavirus second wave a few days before the Sunbelt and West exploded with record cases and hospitals were overwhelmed.

Simultaneously, Trump was busy trying to repeal Obamacare so that millions of Americans who'd lost their jobs would lose their health insurance during a pandemic. I wonder if it came as a surprise to Trump when he found out that his approval rating was dropping so low, former Vice President Joe Biden was beating him in the polls by 14 percent, and some Republicans were floating the idea that Trump should resign—and that was before we found out that he knew Russians were offering bounties to the

Taliban to kill American soldiers, and that he did nothing and then denied that he knew.

Due to the precipitous rise in cases around the country, including Florida (now called Covida), where many New Yorkers have second homes, Governor Cuomo ordered anyone coming from a high corona state to quarantine for two weeks. Broadway postponed reopening from the fall of 2020 until 2021. In case that wasn't enough, Cuomo and Mayor de Blasio were supposedly in talks (those two talked?) about holding off on Phase Three of reopening New York City, which included dining inside with safety restrictions such as 25 percent capacity. That day's headline didn't help matters: "China Researchers Discover New Swine Flu With 'Pandemic Potential.'" I didn't even know it was possible to have more than one pandemic at a time. Did we also need to start getting up to speed on the G4 Virus, which was already on the rise in pig populations? A post pandemic pandemic. Pigdemic anyone? Prepare for more zoonosis.

The louder he talked of his honor,
the faster we counted our spoons.
—RALPH WALDO EMERSON

Chapter 17

A Long, Hot Summer

With no picnics, parades, and fireworks, Independence Day was all but canceled, and people were told to stay home. Granted, there wasn't much to celebrate. However, Trump decided to travel to Mount Rushmore in South Dakota as part of his Make America Sick Again campaign, and have a rally capped off by a fireworks display. In addition to helping spread coronavirus, locals were worried about setting the dry surrounding area ablaze, and Native Americans were calling for the wholesale removal of the Mount Rushmore monument as it was a symbol of treaties broken, Sioux lands appropriated, and murder. While this may have sounded farfetched five months ago, the day before it had been announced that Princeton's Woodrow Wilson School was being renamed, and now a full-page ad in *The New York Times* was calling for Yale to follow. In a reaction to the George Floyd reaction, progressive wish lists were being revisited. The Washington

Redskins owner was doing a "thorough review" of the team name that went back fifty years. Ferret fans in New York City saw it as their chance to get ferret possession made legal after Mayor de Blasio had failed on his campaign promise to reverse Mayor Rudy Giuliani's ferret fatwa. Giuliani had declared that "excessive concern with little weasels is a sickness."

It was just as well I stayed indoors on July 4 since there was plenty of virus homework in the form of theoretical biology as we had to learn about "spike proteins" in "genetic sequencing" along with "antibody therapy." While cases continued to soar across the country, there was now "strong evidence" that a new mutation of the coronavirus had spread from Europe to the US, which was more infectious but did not seem to make people any sicker. Apparently, this new mutation, G614, had almost completely replaced the first version called D614. If that wasn't enough, when I normally would've been enjoying fireworks, this headline appeared on CNN: "A rare case of brain-destroying amoeba has been confirmed in Florida." The Department of Health added, "It's usually fatal." So that was an exciting holiday!

The topper came a day later when *The New York Times* announced, "Bubonic Plague is Diagnosed in China." Next, we were informed that a mysterious DNA strand linked to Neanderthals might significantly increase the likelihood of getting a severe case of Covid-19. So in addition to being tested for coronavirus and antibodies, people were ordering rat traps and flooding Ancestry.com with spit samples to check their Neanderthal content.

It transpired that I was the exception when it came to staying in over the July 4 weekend, and more than a few revelers found good times on Fire Island and outside of Manhattan bars. For those with bad hangovers, there was a harsh wake-up call on Monday morning when Guv Dad held a surprise press conference. He chastised the kids for reckless endangerment while scolding Crazy Uncle Donald Trump for dishonest messaging which led to even more bad behavior. We had our lowest Covid numbers since the crisis began, but Guv Dad was having none of it and threatened citations and summonses. As for Crazy Uncle Donald, the kids were instructed not to listen to him, especially when it came to Covid-19, because he was not trafficking in facts. One sensed it was a prelude to the moment when Guv Dad told us that Crazy Uncle Donald would be going away to get the care that he needed.

However, it wasn't just a lack of wearing masks and social distancing that made the holiday weekend stand out. In New York City sixty-four people were shot, and ten of them lost their lives. Mayor Mom blamed it on the coronavirus—people being "penned up for months." I wasn't so sure. After a long, frigid Buffalo winter of being housebound, during which we had no computers or cable TV, and Monopoly games went on for days, we didn't all emerge on the first nice morning with firearms and shoot our neighbors. On the bright side, despite the explosion in murders, the crime rate was down! Evidently it's harder to rob people when they're at home.

Under the heading of lawlessness, New York City's all-time favorite 1970s pastime was back in a big way. Spray-painted graffiti, or what has since become categorized as "aerosol art," appeared on walls, warehouses, gated storefronts, and of course subway cars, tunnels, and platforms. This time around the messages mostly reflected current concerns about police brutality and coronavirus devastation, but some things remain the same, and many artists just wished to write their names, usually in the form of a recognizable "tag." The only difference was that nowadays you could watch online tutorials about creating and executing your own "tag." Certainly there were more surveillance cameras than fifty years ago, but mandatory masks made it that much easier to avoid identification.

Inside of cramped homes and apartments, "Mom Rage" was boiling over as women slowly and then suddenly cracked up from the stress of caring for children while working, undergoing job loss or reduced hours, worrying about financial instability, shuttered daycare, remote schooling, managing at-risk elderly parents, and dealing with teenagers wanting to hit the streets for protests. If there was a blowtorch in the kitchen for caramelizing sugar atop crème brûlée, searing steak, and roasting bell papers, now was the time to hide it. While journalists were focused on Americans being "self-radicalized" by conspiracy theories and hoarding AM radios, women were being "self-radicalized" at a much faster rate by dirty dishes, dirty diapers, and dirty laundry.

In many cases, women were sacrificing their own sanity, relationships, and health. One friend broke her hand tripping over a sewer grate while trying to grab a few minutes of exercise and solitude. Her gym had been closed for months, and by the time she finished working and taking care of the household, it was dark outside. A fifty-two-year-old friend broke her wrist playing basketball with her sixteen-year-old, a talented athlete who should've been working out with the varsity team. Another tore a knee muscle attempting a home repair because she was afraid to allow a handyman inside. My eighty-eight-year-old friend broke her hip cleaning the china cabinet because the housekeeper had been unable to come for three months and the dust was driving her crazy.

Eleven percent of Americans seriously considered suicide in June, according to one study, which was double the number from the previous year. The descending darkness was described by some women as the mood swings of pregnancy or postpartum depression times ten, and a situation that involved very little sleep with no breaks. They just rose to the same impossible challenges, collapsed into bed, and were supposed to do it all over again. Pandemic pods formed with other families were supposed to help juggle the many challenges, but adding more personalities at close range often had the opposite effect and made life more stressful.

Alternatively, if you were a teen babysitter with antibodies this was a once-in-a-lifetime chance to become a millionaire over a single summer. Whereas the babysitter was normally handed the list of emergency numbers, in this case he or she was the emergency number.

Allowing the kids to stare at an iPad or play (more) video games wasn't even providing women with the relief they needed. If one had time to check the news (which these caregivers did not), it would have been apparent that the childcare crisis wasn't a priority for the grandparents running our nation. Add to that a bunch of old white male politicians who were busy trying to limit access to women's reproductive health care. There was a warning in all of this: When these women are not so exhausted and can find some clean clothes, we'll be hearing their shouts, and feeling their votes, possibly for the next fifty years. Experts say that since 2012 we've been in fourth-wave feminism, and describe it as a "phase." Well, behold a pink tsunami on the horizon that will be much more than any phase, and rather a transformation in how we live, love, and work. The news was rife with talk of QAnon and conspiracy theories, yet investigative reporters were missing the biggest one of all— women were secretly organizing to run the entire world, only it was much more than a theory.

Others were expressing their cabin fever in meta creative ways. The long lines to enter Trader Joe's worsened as social distancing guidelines allowed only a certain number of customers to shop at the same time. As a result, people waited on sidewalks directly in front of apartment buildings, while the dwellers inside wearied of overhearing overly loud conversations, especially early in the morning. After repeatedly requesting that waiting shoppers lower their voices, neighbors began posting conversation snippets on cardboard signs complete with snarky commentary. Soon they were accompanied by cartoons and not long after that posted as tweets (#TraderJoesLineUWS) and Instagram photos:

Jenny, Whoa! Listen. You don't need a nose job! Your nose looks perfect. WE know because we see you with your mask under your nose. Which makes us think you don't understand science . . . so probably best not to have an elective surgery. But get those sriracha seafood potstickers & cheer up!

Irony led to meta irony.

Bridget—I have to hang up! I'm in front of that building where they listen & put what you say on a sign. I'm sure it will just fall off. I will get the matcha powder, oat milk, and chia seeds. Now hang up! xoxo

This wasn't the only form of outdoor harassment on the rise. With indoor dining curtailed indefinitely, restaurants had extended their outdoor areas and people were meeting their friends for meals in parks and other public places. And members of New York's restless rodent population, having suffered from severe scavenging losses during the winter lockdown, were brazenly approaching al fresco diners.

Meantime, teenagers were trolling Donald Trump by posting fake reviews of his properties on Tripadvisor and similar travel sites. Most said they were continuously approached by hookers, the places made them feel "dirty," a scary man in clown makeup had been seen wandering around, and bedbugs were everywhere.

"There's more."

"Of course there is," Brishen said flatly. It had started badly;
it turned worse and hinted at becoming ruinous.
—GRACE DRAVEN,

Chapter 18

A Slow Burn

On Friday, July 10, the US posted a record 70,000 new coronavirus cases. My husband's sister passed away from Covid-19 in South Africa, which was also experiencing huge caseloads. Europe had successfully flattened their curves and children were heading back to school. Angela Merkel gave a speech and said, "As we are experiencing firsthand, you cannot fight the pandemic with lies and disinformation any more than you can fight it with hate or incitement to hatred." Hmmm, who could she be talking about? And who says that Germans don't have a terrific sense of humor? In a karmic twist, the working-class neighborhood of Corona, Queens had been hit so hard they were thought to be one of the first communities with herd immunity when 68 percent of the residents tested positive for antibodies.

We attended my sister-in-law's funeral via Zoom and wow, was that ever depressing. I know funerals aren't organized for the purpose of merrymaking, but I've been to some good ones, where people laugh and cry, remember the dead, and agree how the departed "Really would've loved this!" Growing up among garrulous Irish Catholics and cat lovers, perhaps I just have high expectations—it can be hard to discern between an Irish wedding and an Irish wake, while nobody has better stories than cat persons. Because of the time difference between New York and Cape Town, South Africa, we had to be seated at the computer in our Zoom shirts by 7:30 a.m. At the funeral home, mourners were several feet apart, dressed in black clothing with black masks, and looked like a terrorist group gathered for instructions about their next bombing. I thought the minister was speaking in Afrikaans (which wouldn't make sense since the family used English) but then realized it was just bad audio combined with a South African accent. Our niece carried her laptop outside so we could watch the casket be lifted into the hearse while hearing unidentified sobs. The hearse drove off into the gloom and the red "leave meeting" appeared. Amen, I guess.

In mid-July we entered the inferno stage of our journey. The country was experiencing a dangerous heat wave affecting fifty million people. The East Coast buckled under a series of 95°F plus days while Phoenix, another virus hotspot, hit 116°F. Death Valley, California, reached 127°F, so they came by their name honestly. The number of new Covid cases in Florida (15,300) topped New York's worst days back in April, but Disney World went ahead and reopened anyway. Staff and visitors had their temperatures taken, but in 100-degree heat I'm not sure how well that works if the outside air is hotter than your insides are supposed to be. Similarly, many other parts of the country were experiencing huge spikes in the virus while New York had its first day with not a single death from Covid-19 since the whole nightmare began. Some red state politicians could even be heard saying that they needed to handle the situation "like New York."

The virus was surging or resurging in cities across the nation and it was hard to think New York City wouldn't be next with all our airports and train and bus stations. The end of July became a flurry of appointments—basically anything and everything you could think of, plus whatever you needed done on the house or apartment in case of another lockdown. Experts were nattering on about a Second Wave, so we all wanted to dine outside at least once prior to being locked up again. I had dinner with a friend on Amsterdam Avenue as fire engines and motorcycles roared past. My friend was in the high-risk category due to age and preexisting conditions, and thus trying out her clear plastic face shield for the first time—only it was so clear that she kept putting food on the visor rather than in her mouth. I was reminded of birds who fly into glass windows. Nature was definitely having her revenge.

It wasn't encouraging when Chicago cases began rising, and it was downright frightening when a Colorado squirrel tested positive for bubonic plague, and health officials warned the disease can be transmitted to humans and pets if "proper precautions" aren't taken. So add squirrel avoidance to our ever-growing list of safeguards. Get all the peanuts out of your pockets, everyone. On the bright side, the next day it was announced that the studies from a few months back about people with Type A blood being more likely to get the virus and to become more dangerously ill than others, well, those were out the window. Have any blood type you want.

Meanwhile, Republicans were plowing ahead with their convention, which had gone from Charlotte, NC, to a large venue in Jacksonville, FL, to being scaled back and incorporating outdoor locations in Jacksonville. Most Republican congresspersons over seventy-five suddenly remembered something else they had to do. Others passed at the last minute like it was a high school party that sounded good until, just before heading out the door, you heard the parents were going to be home.

Cases kept rising, and Trump and the Republicans kept pushing back against science, even as they contracted the virus. The administration trashed Dr. Anthony Fauci, but he popped up like the principal taking over the class for a teacher who has lost control of the room and announced, "Let's stop this nonsense" in a very no-nonsense voice. Everyone at the White House, including the president, insisted they hadn't been the ones attacking Dr. Fauci. And most Republican governors finally told their constituents to wear masks. But not Kevin Stitt in Oklahoma. Stitt posted an Instagram photo of himself with his family inside a crowded restaurant and attended Trump's Tulsa super-spreader rally, became the first governor to contract coronavirus, and then claimed he was "pretty shocked." Just like Buffalonians would be shocked to get frostbite after going sledding in a bikini and flip-flops in March.

The newspaper story titled "Study Suggests Virus Can Be Passed to Fetus" felt like it should be on the front page, but in this never-ending horror film that was our daily lives had been buried inside, because that's how gothic things had gotten. The next day it was announced that eighty-five infants under the age of one had tested positive for coronavirus in Nueces County, Texas. That was quickly followed by "Texas Hospital Says Man, 30, Died After Attending A 'Covid Party' With an Infected Person to See if It Was Real." Texas was definitely making news. This is the kind of headline we'd come to expect from Florida, only it would involve alligator wrestling.

The Zoom memorial service for my sister-in-law was held on Sunday, July 20, and it wasn't nearly as depressing as the funeral. However, the following morning we received news that my husband's cousin had succumbed to Covid-19. The outbreak of coronavirus in the southern and western United States was increasing at an alarming rate, while places thought to have "flattened the curve," like Ohio, were smoldering enough to indicate that a resurgence was afoot. Fox News ran an interview of Donald Trump saying how well he was doing at combating the virus.

Many states governed by Republicans had adopted a "Live Free or Die" motto as their health care policy. On Monday morning, House Speaker Nancy Pelosi went on national television to say that Republicans who were complicit in the president's irresponsibility were going to have dog poop on their shoes that was going to smell for a very long time. Leave it to Nana Nancy to frame the response to a pandemic in terms even a kindergarten class could understand.

When a stupid government is elected in a democratic country, the best thing about this is that you learn the number of stupid people in that country!

—MEHMET MURAT İLDAN

Chapter 19

The Knucklehead Dilemma

New York City entered "Phase Four" of the reopening process, only without opening indoor dining or enclosed gathering spaces such as museums, theaters, and malls. Bars serving booze out front had created a clever work-around to the requirement that food had to be purchased along with alcohol, and were selling Cuomo Chips with salsa for one dollar. Covid speakeasies had popped up around the city, away from the prying eyes of law enforcement. Add to that we were in our second week of the heat index cracking one hundred. This led to overcrowding and over-reveling, and Gov Dad was *really* mad, once again. He'd received another secret stash of photos showing rulebreakers in Astoria. Being a Queens native, Cuomo took them to task in their own accent: "Knock it off, don't be stupid." Guv Dad threatened to shut it all right back down. Then he tried some common sense: "Even if you're in your twenties you can get sick. And you can make other people sick." For good measure he tacked on a Dad catchphrase, "You're not a super-hero, but you could become a super-spreader." Just so you didn't mistake that for a joke, or think Guv Dad wasn't taking names, he suspended the liquor license of four bars and restaurants—three in Queens and one on Long Island. This was in addition to the 410 charges against establishments for violating executive orders and twenty-seven previously suspended licenses.

Guv Dad wasn't finished after straightening out the kids. Crazy Uncle Donald threatened to send federal troops to New York to deal with protesters aka "anarchists who hate our country" (who is the "our" in that sentence?) like he'd done in Portland (which resulted in much more violence). Guv Dad told Crazy Uncle Donald to check his medication and take another cognitive test, and we all knew that meant if Guv Dad saw so much as one person in camouflage on lower Broadway, Crazy Uncle Donald would wake up with a horse head in his White House bed (on top of the cheeseburger wrappers and Diet Coke cans).

California overtook New York State for the total number of coronavirus cases on July 23, 2020, which finally ended our number one Hot Zone status. And at the rate Texas and Florida were going, they'd soon surpass our number two slot when it came to the highest Covid caseload in the country. Lo and behold, Trump abruptly caved into the reality of the disease and cancelled the portion of the Republican Party Convention scheduled to take place in Jacksonville, Florida.

Guv Dad, not wanting to regain our leading virus status, penned a "Dear Kids" letter that began, "I have a message for young people: This is not the time to fight for your right to party," and ended with, "If you treat

COVID lightly, you may not live to regret it." Subtle. The punishment: no more Cuomo Chips. Going forward, alcoholic beverages had to be accompanied by a "substantial item." On Friday afternoon he was back: "Wear a mask. And twenty somethings—this means you." Then he went after their dealers by announcing that the State Liquor Authority had issued thirty-seven violations the previous night, and establishments faced fines of up to $10,000 per violation. "Business owners: Don't risk it." We were all "on notice" as Dads like to say, and I certainly didn't want to get grounded and have to clean out my drawers.

Cuomo was doing well with the tough talk and his approval rating continued to soar. However, he picked one wrong fight, not with Trump over sending in federal troops, but with Buffalo when he declared chicken wings didn't count as "substantial food." Upon having this staple in their local diet attacked, western New Yorkers declared that Cuomo had become a monarch. The Governor and his team quickly walked back the bad wing call and insisted wings *are* on the substantive food list. Sorry chickens.

Despite the food fights, New York was showing safer signs of life. Major League Baseball reopened with the Washington Nationals playing the New York Yankees in the Bronx (without fans in attendance) to four million viewers. Prior to the game, every player and coach held up a black banner that stretched along the first and third baselines, then took a knee in silence for Black Lives Matter. Following that, Dr. Fauci threw out a first pitch that turned out to be extremely socially distanced from the catcher. In fact, it was so far off base that one Twitter wag noted, "He clearly doesn't want anyone to catch anything." Fauci said he had gone to a high school a few days prior to play catch for the first time in decades and injured his throwing arm in private practice. No matter, opening day euphoria lasted exactly forty-eight hours until games were postponed due to a coronavirus outbreak among the Miami Marlins players, staff, and coaches. The day after that, the Phillies postponed their (second) game against the Yankees.

This was followed by another installment in the Florida vs. New York saga (the Sunshine State had attempted to ban us from visiting, and three months later The Empire State added *them* to our quarantine list). On July 25, Florida overtook New York for the number two spot of the most Covid cases. But we figured that had happened at least a month ago, since Florida was using some swampy math to cook the coronavirus books and make it appear as if they'd had fewer cases all along. Still, it was a friendly, if deadly, competition since Miami is known as the last stop on the Long Island Railroad, and you're just as likely to hear a New York accent in Palm Beach as you are in, well, New York.

Gov Dad was indeed having a tough summer among an ongoing heat wave, trying to keep the virus from surging on his turf, and catching flack for how he'd handled nursing home cases early in the pandemic. Finally, he went after the grownups, who were supposed to be acting responsibly, but instead led the whole neighborhood astray. No gatherings of more than fifty people were allowed. Yet, a Hamptons dance party with two thousand attendees had Guv Dad "appalled by egregious social distancing." They argued that the money raised was going to charity, but Gov Dad was having none of it, and like any father who used to work in law enforcement, announced he was launching his own investigation with help from his old pals in the Health Department. It reminded me of my friend Mary's dad, who'd stayed busy grounding his nine children for various lengths of time, and during a particularly raucous summer just grounded everyone until September.

Next up to bat was responsible Uncle Phil Murphy, Governor of New Jersey. After local officers couldn't break up a rager of seven hundred and the state police had to be called in, Uncle Phil went on television and warned future party planners, "Stay out of the knucklehead hall of fame." Still, I think both East Coast Guvs were jealous when Los Angeles Mayor Eric Garcetti threatened to cut off the water and power for any residents holding house parties or operating what he called "nightclubs in the hills."

The number crunchers were back to using war analogies, and on July 27, 2020, coronavirus deaths in the US surpassed the number of Union Army soldiers killed on battlefields during the Civil War. Speaking of death, nearly three thousand small businesses in New York City had closed for good over the previous four months due to falling revenue, vanished tourism, and burgeoning debt, particularly from overdue rent. Dealing with the continuous and heartbreaking loss of life was almost impossible, and then I'd walk through what had recently been vibrant, thriving New York City neighborhoods that now resembled the hollowed out Rust Belt factory towns of my youth. Where was the hope? I had to admit that I'd lost my optimism that life would ever return to normal, and was no longer sure that we'd even survive all of this.

As more states were added to New York's quarantine list, and Canada still had a big KEEP OUT sign on its front lawn, New Yorkers were forced to vacation in New York. Having driven from Buffalo to the east end of Long Island, I was aware it's a big state (compared to the New Yorkers who think Rochester is an hour or two away—just head north and make your first left). I knew the state east to west but had no idea what was happening up north, so I drove five hours up to Plattsburgh and was amazed to see there is a whole world with people living, working, and going to optometrists the same as we did. They just have more space, are for the most part friendlier, and are considerably colder for half of the year. I saw Lake Schroon and Lake George for the first time, and Lake Placid—so that's where they held the 1980 winter Olympics I'd watched on television.

I'm embarrassed about this next admission, but I'd never been to the Adirondacks, which is 160 miles in diameter, covers one fifth of the state, is three times the size of Yellowstone Park, and equal in size to Vermont. All I knew about the Adirondacks is that Teddy Roosevelt was hiking there when President William McKinley was assassinated at the Pan-American Exposition in Buffalo back in 1901, and someone had to run up a mountain and fetch him. Imagine my surprise when I learned that Adirondack State Park contains dozens of towns and villages along with farms, Pilates studios, and timber harvesting. And with more than ten thousand lakes and thirty thousand miles of rivers and streams at their disposal, kayakers and fisherpersons aren't jockeying for space. But good luck finding a place to hide from the bloodsucking mosquitoes and black flies.

Miraculously, the Covid numbers in New York remained low, while the rest of the country continued to break records; the US death toll passed 150,000, more than one fifth of the world's deaths. This was fifty times the death toll on 9/11, but didn't seem to merit one tenth the urgency of 9/11 from our government. Cases were surging in California and the Southeast, while the Midwest developed hotspots and was expected to grow much worse. Crazy Uncle Donald was reported to have said, "Now our people are getting it!" Meaning what—Republicans? Idiots? Indeed, the first few months the virus had largely devasted cities, which are democratic strongholds of god-less, smoothie-swilling progressives.

Congressman Louie Gohmert, who forbade his staff from wearing masks and discouraged his constituents from doing so, tested positive for coronavirus. The Texas Republican went so far as to say that his mask had *caused him* to get coronavirus, even though it had been scientifically proven that wearing a mask was the easiest way not to spread or contract coronavirus. My mother the nurse said of Gohmert, "Some people have to learn the hard way." Then Gohmert attempted to quarantine in his office at the Capitol rather than get a hotel room.

Hong Kong is the densest city in the world, and they'd done a remarkable job of stopping Covid by everyone wearing masks. With a population equivalent to that of New York City, Hong Kong had 11,000 cases to our 700,000, and 197 deaths to our 29,000. How does one argue with that? But there was Crazy Uncle Donald, mask-less while holding a fundraiser in Texas. His message to donors, in addition to there being no need for masks, was that he'd passed legislation to stop Black people from moving to the suburbs and ruining everything. He was also calling on "the housewives" to support him.

Trump's dog whistles had become ferocious barks, and his blind followers followed. Georgia Republican Senator David Perdue ran an ad that enlarged the nose of his Jewish opponent, Democrat Jon Ossoff. This photoshopped image was placed above the caption, "Democrats Are Trying to Buy Georgia." The campaign blamed it on an error. Of course, that happens to me all the time when I'm taking photos at weddings and the noses keep coming out the wrong size. In the other Georgia Senate runoff, Republican Kelly Loeffler's Facebook ad against her Black opponent Raphael Warnock also had faulty photoshopping; Warnock's skin had been darkened. Republican senator Lindsay Graham from South Carolina was having similar camera problems in his race against African American Democrat Jaime Harrison. In Graham's political ads, Harrison's skin also appeared darker.

Only idiots are confident. It requires a great amount
of wisdom and knowledge to be confused.

—ABHISHEK LEELA PANDEY

Chapter 20

Caught in a Storm

On July 30, we awoke to a news trifecta: The economy
had shrunk by record numbers (despite the government
having pumped in trillions of dollars), the coronavirus case
total in Texas surpassed that of New York, and Herman
Cain died of Covid-19. The former Republican presidential candidate tested positive for the virus after attending
Trump's super-spreader indoor rally in Tulsa without wearing a mask or social distancing.

Crazy Uncle Donald's response to all of this was to
suggest delaying the election in hopes of shoring up his
cratering approval ratings and poll numbers (and so he'd
get to hold off those prosecutors and remain Idiot in Chief
a little longer even if he did eventually lose). Making the
day all the more surreal, he was referring to Yosemite
National Park as "Yo! Semite" on national television. I
recalled the high school chant shouted at visiting teams
who were losing: "Warm up the bus! Warm up the bus!"

But then former First Lady Michelle Obama revealed that she was suffering from depression, which served to depress the rest of us.

Still, we definitely should've seen this next one coming as the writing was on the empty dressing room walls: Companies that sold pants declared bankruptcy or went out of business, including Lord & Taylor, J. Crew, Brooks Brothers, Century 21, and Tailored Brands (parent of Men's Warehouse and Jos. A Bank chains). With interest rates at zero, now was the time to put all your pants in a safety deposit box; surely they'd be valuable as soon as a vaccine was discovered. Or possibly as antiques in a decade or so.

It was just as well the pants were gone since a hurricane barreled up the East Coast, and pants would have only slowed us down. Someone named it Isaias just to be annoying. I understand the desire for storm diversity but what happened to Jorge and Isobel? A hurricane name is something you need to say time and again for the rest of your life when exchanging stories about it. I can only imagine if Buffalo's Blizzard of '77 had been called Grzegorz or Kazimierz. Hurricane Isaias, with wind gusts of seventy mph, caused power failures along with flash flooding throughout the Northeast, and New York had its second worst outage since Superstorm Sandy in 2012. The emergency was a repeat of the coronavirus in the sense that utility workers had to come from all over the country to help us. Still, it took almost a week to restore power in many parts of the city, while the temperature sailed right back to 85°F with hair curling humidity.

After the power failure I thought that I needed my eyes checked. When the lights came back on, Liberty University President and rabid Trump supporter Jerry Falwell Jr. had popped up again, so to speak. He'd posted a photo of himself on a yacht, holding a beverage, with his pants open and unzipped, midriff exposed, and his arm around a scantily clad younger woman (not his wife). Pantsgate! Liberty's board of trustees requested the evangelical Christian leader "take an indefinite leave of absence." This was an hour after US intelligence officials announced that Russia was continuing to interfere in our elections to boost Trump, so if Falwell meant to distract from that, he did a good job. Clearly the two were in cahoots, since at the same time, Crazy Uncle Donald was saying, "Thighland" instead of "Thailand." A new adjective was becoming popular for people misbehaving in the age of coronavirus—"Covidiots."

It didn't exactly help the national mood when the news showed pictures of massive pool parties in Wuhan, China, and reported the city was back to normal with virus transmission near zero. Needless to say, we didn't receive any invitations. Americans were still prohibited from traveling to China or Europe, while Canada had just extended their ban on us for another month. I wondered how they'd survive without Fluffernutter. When I was a kid, Frostbacks were always popping across the border to load up on Fluff and VCR movies.

Our houses are such unwieldy property that
we are often imprisoned rather than housed in them.
—HENRY DAVID THOREAU,

Chapter 21

Nowhere to Run, No Place to Hide

I t was the 75th anniversary of the US dropping atomic bombs on Hiroshima and Nagasaki, which lead to the end of World War II. However, in real time, a huge explosion in Beirut, Lebanon, killed at least 204 people, caused 6,500 injuries, and destroyed entire neighborhoods. It was believed to be the result of government negligence, and protests erupted among Lebanese citizens exasperated by corrupt leaders and oligarchs. In Europe, the people of Belarus rose up against their dictator of the past twenty-six years, Alexander Lukashenko. In West Africa, Mali's President and Prime Minister were arrested in a coup. All big news, and yet, with the complete and total chaos in the US, it was hard to turn one's attention to history or any other part of the world.

Vladimir Putin announced on August 11 that Russia had won the race to develop an effective coronavirus vaccine. You'd have thought the Dow Jones Average would've soared on such news, but it went down one hundred points. We were thinking "Russian roulette" and that Americans wouldn't exactly be lining up to get a Vlad vax. Meantime, our own autocrat was busy sabotaging the US Post Office. If you couldn't mail your ballot then there couldn't be an election, or at the very least the result would be thrown into chaos for years to come.

On August 17, a banner appeared over Ocean Grove, NJ, with the *cri de guerre*: JOIN THE BATTLE—BEAT THE BUG. There was a picture of an insect with black-dotted crimson and gray wings called a "spotted lanternfly." Officials from the state's Department of Agriculture placed eight counties under quarantine while asking travelers through the area to check for "hitchhiking bugs" and "eliminate" them if you're "able to." I am not making this up—we were indeed revisiting the pestilence chapter of our doomsday Bible just eight short weeks after the murder hornet alarms went off. This newly discovered inch-long pest was menacing the Northeast, intent upon destroying crops, particularly vineyards. And if a few lanternflies managed to catch an Amtrak or Greyhound to Napa Valley, everyone was going to be sipping Mello Yello in their pandemic pods. Space aliens had to be coming next. How could they not be?

There was still no indoor dining in New York City, and it became hard to tell if the asphalt was a bus lane, turn lane, bike path, ConEdison work site, or outdoor restaurant. Several dining establishments that had turned al fresco actually incorporated preexisting bus shelters into their "streeteries," and you couldn't be sure if a couple was waiting for drinks and apps or the 79th Street crosstown bus. However, with such a large percentage of coronavirus cases in the tri-state area, we all breathed a collective sigh of relief when the Centers for Disease

Control and Prevention (CDC) announced that a person who had recovered from Covid-19 would likely be safe from reinfection for three months. Two weeks later they backtracked on that guidance. The next day Donald Trump's younger brother Robert died in New York City of . . . it was a mystery. Coronavirus anyone?

The following day offered this news flash: "Scientists who have been monitoring immune responses to the coronavirus for months are now starting to see encouraging signs of strong, lasting immunity, even in people that developed only mild symptoms of Covid-19, a flurry of new studies has found." Meanwhile, we had two new covocabulary words— "twindemic" was employed to describe the Category 5 Shitshow bearing down on us as Covid was about to collide with flu season, while "double masking" was your best and perhaps only hope for survival.

The pandemic carousel continued spinning, and wherever she stopped it became increasingly obvious we weren't winning. It was unclear how New Yorkers could be more stressed out as we anxiously awaited the dreaded Second Wave—until it became crystal clear when New York City Police Department's union endorsed President Trump in his race for a second term. It was the first time they'd endorsed a candidate in at least thirty-six years. New York has a Democratic governor, Democratic majority in the state legislature, Democratic mayor in New York City, and city residents vote 70 percent Democratic. Manhattan dogs wear blue designer sweaters. Was this part of the PD's community policing plan? Add "revanchism" to the vocabulary list.

In addition to the relentless heat wave, August brought a variety of apocalyptic weather events. Iowa experienced a fourteen-hour land hurricane (or "derecho") that damaged homes, farms, crops, schools, and businesses to the tune of about $4 billion. Winds topping 105 miles per hour knocked out power to a million plus Midwesterners. In California, over 580 wildfires were burning, many of them sparked by lightning, and a series of "fire tornadoes" had developed from the intense temperatures and high wind speeds. Even professional weather forecasters found themselves Googling "firenado" in real time. At least a dozen people died, a hundred thousand were evacuated, and air quality was dangerously poor. The dire situation also wreaked havoc on coronavirus testing in the state, which was still home to a large number of hotspots. Residents were said to be suffering from "disaster dissonance" because they were supposed to be *outside* to avoid contracting Covid, yet abysmal air quality had forced them *inside*.

In the Southeast, two tropical storms, Marco and Laura, advanced on the Gulf of Mexico. Meteorologists were doing backflips because it was the first time the Gulf might have two hurricanes simultaneously. My mom was excited because a potentially memorable storm had finally been named after me. The horror shows playing out on the Weather Channel rather overshadowed the fact that our mail was arriving days and sometimes more than a week and a half late. (But you definitely noticed if you were one of the many people depending on mail delivery for medication and pension checks.) While we were roasting in the hot sun with our masks on, and battening down the hatches for another hurricane, Crazy Uncle Donald—afraid of losing the upcoming presidential election—was accused of instructing his handpicked Postmaster General henchman to not just slow down mail delivery, but to remove our mailboxes. Because people who didn't want to die of coronavirus planned to vote by mail, he figured that by gumming up the works, he could declare the election was rigged and thus become a dictator. The "restructuring" aka sabotage also included removing thousands of mail sorting machines (some brand new), limiting overtime, and reducing post office hours and delivery trips.

People who order live baby ducks, geese, and chickens through the mail were also experiencing a grave problem, which you can probably surmise. Likewise, rent and mortgage payments weren't getting to their destinations on time, so late fees were charged or eviction proceedings initiated. And if kids wished to send a letter to Santa, they were advised to have it in the mail by Labor Day.

Yes, we speak of things that matter
With words that must be said
"Can analysis be worthwhile?"
"Is the theater really dead?"
—Simon & Garfunkel,
"The Dangling Conversation," 1966

Chapter 22

Stop Spreading the News

Another of Trump's crooked cronies popped up trying to sell the public on another fake coronavirus cure. My Pillow CEO Mike Lindell was trumpeting an untested plant extract as "the miracle of all time." There were no studies showing that his oleandrin worked on coronavirus, yet it had been proved that ingesting a tiny bit of the oleander shrub can kill you. Anyone who ever read a mystery novel knew that oleander is used to murder people (and commit suicide). *White Oleander* anyone? While we're on the subject, don't ever toast marshmallows on an oleander branch, advises this former camp counselor.

Elsewhere, there was something bubbling in the news about using plasma from people who'd tested positive for coronavirus as a remedy. Supposedly the Food and Drug

Administration (FDA) was pressured by Trump to prematurely approve it without sufficient testing and despite
concerns by government doctors and scientists. Who
knew, who cared. Bring back leaches. I didn't even have
the energy to Google the words "convalescent plasma."
However, I heard that this probable boondoggle had
created some new jobs—cold calling patients who'd had
Covid to ask for a plasma donation—a new variety of
telemarketer, indeed. At the same time, Russia supposedly proved their "vaccine" worked, but nobody believed
them, especially since Crazy Uncle Donald's bestie Mad
Vlad had just poisoned another one of his own political
rivals a day earlier. Add these corona conundrums to the
concurrent headline in *The New York Times* magazine
asking, "To Control Covid-19, Would It Help if America
Started Using Less-Accurate Tests?" Seriously, I was getting a headache. It quickly turned into a migraine when a
patient in Hong Kong was diagnosed with a second case
of Covid-19 four months after her first one by real doctors
and scientists.

The whole pandemic had become far worse than most
dystopian fiction horror films or political thrillers. It was
more confounding than reading a book about the family
of American author Henry James and his brother William,
wherein everyone is named Henry or William, and after a
few chapters you've completely lost the plot and your mind.

As New York's virus numbers continued to drop, we
saw reports that a non-Russian vaccine could be ready as
soon as January, and were astonished. Until now it had
felt like month after month of bad news being followed
by worse news, such as when *The Atlantic* announced
that wild animals harbor an estimated 40,000 unknown
viruses, a quarter of which could potentially jump into
humans. Right after that there was a pepperoni shortage.

In New York City, an exhausted and heat-scorched citizenry, especially those with compromised immune systems, was increasingly challenged by the antics of anti-maskers. The issue had caused so many physical altercations that the CDC issued an official decree warning retail and service employees not to argue with rule breakers. Apparently fist fights could be hazardous to your health. A more complex issue was what to do about the many people who did wear masks, but pulled them down below their mouths every time they wanted to say or shout something, especially when riding buses and subways, or while standing in lobbies and elevators.

The city that supposedly never sleeps was now in a coma. People who'd fled to summer homes were apparently never coming back. The exodus was so abrupt that moving companies were said to be turning customers away. Many workers would continue to operate online at least through January and possibly forever. Landlords were offering unheard of discounts while retail spaces sat empty and office leases expired. Trash piled up in city parks and playgrounds due to budget cuts. The MTA was destitute with ridership at one tenth of what it had been, and in worse shape than during the Great Depression. There were echoes of the 1970s and 80s as homeless encampments sprung up and violent crime skyrocketed. Broadway had no reopening date. One still could not go to a movie or visit a gym or eat inside a restaurant. Teachers worried about returning to school in September and threatened a "sick out."

The former New Yorker who occupied the Oval Office was noticeably unsympathetic, and the famous 1975 *Daily News* headline came to mind, only this time it would read: "Trump to City: Drop Dead". Some business owners went so far as to describe the situation as a death spiral. Of course, longtime New Yorkers had read our obituary several times by now, but that didn't mean it wasn't difficult and discouraging.

On Monday, August 24, the day millions of children around the country started online school, there were major Zoom outages and lots of happy kids (and suicidal parents). I think we'd just discovered the 21st century version of academic sabotage. Back in my day kids had to sneak inside the bus depot and put sugar in the gas tanks to cancel school. As my friend's prescient teen daughter explained to me, the worst thing about remote schooling was there'd be no more snow days.

On Tuesday, August 25, the CDC announced changes in its testing guidelines—this after pressure from Crazy Uncle Donald to test less so it'd appear that fewer people had coronavirus. The CDC held the meeting about the decision while Dr. Fauci was under anesthetic for surgery on his vocal cords. The new recommendation said you did *not* need a test after being exposed to someone with coronavirus. New York Governor Andrew Cuomo's head exploded and he said, "Shame on the people of the CDC. This will not look well in the scope of the history. What plausible rationale would say, 'if you're in close contact with a person who has COVID, you don't need a test.'"

In other cuckoo Covid news, FDA Commissioner and court magician Dr. Stephen Hahn apologized for "overselling" plasma's benefits as a coronavirus treatment after withering criticism from doctors and scientists. Let's just say we saw that one coming. Or, as my New York neighbor summed it up, "Plasma Shmasma." Still, it certainly raised the question of how many people would be willing to get a "coronavirus vaccine" touted by the current administration.

On Wednesday, August 26, just about every professional sports team canceled their game to protest the shooting of twenty-nine-year-old Jacob Blake in Kenosha, WI. The NBA, WNBA, Major League Baseball, Major League Soccer, and the professional tennis tour all came to a screeching halt after having risked their lives to train and play during coronavirus. Blake is a Black man who was shot seven times in the back by a white police officer as he was getting into his car, where his three young children were. Protests by day turned to looting and violence at night, during which two people were killed and a third was seriously wounded. A group of men carrying guns, including military-style semiautomatic weapons, who said they were there to protect businesses, engaged with a crowd. A seventeen-year-old from Illinois shot three protesters (killing two) and was arrested for first degree intentional homicide. Video showed the perpetrator, Kyle Rittenhouse, had been in the front row of a Des Moines Trump rally on January 30.

After several surgeries, Jacob Blake was still in the hospital and partially paralyzed. That same night, Vice President Pence spoke at the Republican National Convention about needing to restore law and order to our cities. Pence was the guy who in 2017 flew to Indianapolis for an NFL game at taxpayer expense for the sole purpose of walking out after several players knelt during the national anthem to express their distress over police brutality. Meantime, Trump's Attorney General Bill Barr denied any systemic racism existed in our society.

Coronavirus had by now officially killed over 180,000 Americans. California continued burning, but there was no room for that on the news. Late Wednesday night Hurricane Laura struck the coasts of Texas and Louisiana at 150 mph, leaving over half a million without power, thousands homeless, and businesses in ruins. A chemical fire erupted near Louisiana's Lake Charles in the aftermath. Local residents who still had functioning homes were told to turn off their air-conditioners (it was 90°F). Since the area was already hard hit by Covid, local health experts were calling it a "crisis within a crisis."

On Thursday, August 27, the director of the CDC *changed his mind* and said that those who'd come in contact with someone who might have Covid could indeed be tested, even if they weren't showing symptoms. That evening, Crazy Uncle Donald declared, "I profoundly accept this nomination for president" on the South Lawn of the White House where roughly 1,500 people were packed in with no social distancing, few masks, and Rudy Giuliani sweating profusely. At the same time as our nation's top coronavirus and climate denier was spewing an alternate reality, the Pine Gulch Fire became the largest wildfire in Colorado history, scorching 139,006 acres in the western part of the state.

On Friday, August 28, those who'd attended the largely maskless Republican National Convention in Charlotte, North Carolina, were already testing positive for coronavirus. That afternoon the first case of coronavirus reinfection was confirmed in the United States, and was the first in the world known to present with severe symptoms. The patient was a twenty-five-year-old man in Reno, Nevada, who experienced the second bout of infection just forty-eight days after the first.

On Saturday, August 29, Portland, Oregon, was having one of its nightly protests since the killing of George Floyd in Minneapolis. A caravan of Trump supporters traveled through the city clashing with protesters, and a white man was shot and killed. Trumpsters shot paintballs from trucks and Black Lives Matter supporters threw objects, while some of the conflicts devolved into fistfights.

And that is what a single week was like in the summer of 2020. The Department of Health and Human Services announced it was spending $250 million to "defeat despair and inspire hope." Apparently DHHS staff had also been watching the news. How much is that in rainbows and lollipops?

All I can say about September 1 is that it felt way too much like April 1, especially as New York City schools delayed their opening by ten days, while colleges and college towns around the country were seeing daily Covid spikes, with many forced to revert back to remote learning. Experts suggested we were suffering from collective "coronasomnia"—that the pandemic had created a massive new population of chronic insomniacs struggling with declines in productivity, shorter fuses, and increased risks of hypertension, depression, and other health problems. Turning on the TV brought poignant appeals from plucky and adorable kids fighting cancer at St. Jude's Hospital, tear-inducing WWF pleas to save the polar bears, fat-shaming weight loss company come-ons, and a heartbreaking ASPCA montage of adorable dogs and cats who'd suffered abuse. I suppose it was comforting to know that I wasn't the only one awake in the middle of the night searching for news stories saying that this would all be over by tomorrow. I had stopped Googling "Broadway reopening" months ago.

The CDC told public health officials around the country to prepare to distribute "the vaccine" as soon as the end of October. And I hope it also said to prepare plenty of storage space because those wouldn't be flying off the shelves. Coronavirus Halloween costumes were going to be more popular than a vaccine touted by Crazy Uncle Donald, the bleach-injecting flimflammer in chief.

Labor Day weekend was filled with directives to wear facial coverings and avoid parties. Instead of sales on linens, store windows advertised "Buy one mask, get one free!" Police and protesters were still clashing across the country as more videos of excessive force against black people were made public. Most recently, Rochester, New York, had joined the conflagration. The West was burning with new wildfires. People fled their homes while campers were rescued after being trapped in the Sierra National Forest. Shortly after that a pyrotechnic device used at a gender reveal celebration ignited the El Dorado fire that caused twenty-one thousand people to evacuate and consumed thousands of acres east of Los Angeles. (It was a boy.) Oregon and Washington were next with thousands of homes burned to the ground—entire communities destroyed by wildfires. Oregon officials warned the populace to prepare for a "mass fatality incident," which sounded like a euphemism for DOOM. The fiery skies, dark haze, and ashes falling like snowflakes had people calling it a "nuclear winter." Others said it looked like Mars. Speaking of Mars, I wondered if there was any update on whether the Red Planet would support human life . . . soon. Crazy Uncle Donald insisted that climate change was a "hoax," just like he'd said about Russian interference in our elections and the coronavirus, which would eventually kill over half a million Americans.

If that wasn't excitement enough, a paramilitary militia calling themselves the Wolverine Watchmen were plotting to kidnap, torture, and kill the Democratic Governor of Michigan, Gretchen Whitmer, and then violently overthrow the state government. Next stop was a second Civil War.

No one could fault the group for not having goals. The FBI eventually caught up with all of them—at least we hoped they had. However, Trump had supported the state's protests against Covid measures, disparaging Governor Whitmer as "that woman from Michigan" and tweeted "LIBERATE MICHIGAN." These far-right groups wanted their "freedom," yet when it came to taking a knee at a ball game, no one was supposed to have the freedom to do that. Go figure. Why have stop signs—let's all be free!

This place is like Dr. Seuss's worst nightmare!

—ROCKHOUND IN

Chapter 23

Worst Halloween Movie Ever

B ob Woodward's book *Rage* revealed that Crafty Uncle Donald had actually known how deadly the pandemic was since back in January, but chose to mislead 332 million Americans by intentionally downplaying the virus (and continued to do so) while discouraging mitigation strategies (and continued to do so). He also knew that coronavirus was airborne, at least five times deadlier than the flu, and that it attacked children as well as adults. But he chose to do little about it, such as ramping up the production of protective gear and testing supplies, except hold massive rallies that turned into super-spreader events.

Moreover, the President of our country liked to announce that children were "almost immune" from coronavirus even though a million had tested positive. He lied because he didn't want the stock market to go down and hurt his reelection chances, and the people who worked with him knew but chose complicity, so as to remain in his good graces, rather than tell the public the truth. There it was in his own recorded, date-stamped words—what the President knew and when he knew it. So much for learning in school that the president's number one job was to protect the American people.

Schools continued to report thousands of new coronavirus cases across the country. Some closed while others soldiered on, with kids bringing the virus home to their families. A teacher friend returned to his high school in October after having last been in the classroom on Friday, March 13. It happened that he'd been teaching *Great Expectations* by Charles Dickens and said the situation could best be described in Miss Havisham terms—it was almost Halloween, but he came back to rooms full of St. Patrick's Day decorations, now all tattered, discolored, and decaying. He checked for uneaten cake on the desktops.

Halloween costumes (we already had masks) and candy popped up in storefronts. But it only served to make everyone sad. Why? For what? *The Wall Street Journal* asked, "Can You Trust a Trick-or-Treater?" When I was growing up kids worried about being harmed by the people giving out candy—that it could contain poison or razor blades, but now homeowners were afraid of being killed by children in costumes. My husband and I canceled the Thanksgiving gathering we'd hosted the past twenty-five years. Christmas was next on the list. New Year's Eve at home, anyone? Time was no longer measured in months or seasons, but in coronavirus waves.

If that wasn't bad enough, Mom and Dad were fighting again. Mayor de Blasio didn't like Governor Cuomo's plan to restart indoor dining in New York City, and wanted a later opening date with a firm requirement to shut down if infection rates rose. De Blasio said a deal was in the works, but Cuomo went ahead and made the announcement without him.

Schools were opening. The neighborhood was suddenly filled with cars, kids, strollers, dogs, food trucks, and people rushing to work. For the first time in months it took time for the elevator to arrive, and now there were actually other humans riding it. I'd somehow forgotten we lived in a throbbing metropolis, and not a small town where the big event of the day was the mail arrival. I'd forgotten about seniors yelling at young people on scooters weaving in and out of pedestrian traffic, and harried parents arguing over taxicabs during the morning rush hour so their children wouldn't be late for school. My husband complained about a phalanx of intruders at his beloved Starbucks, the place where everyone knew his name (at five different locations).

Adding to the wildfires in California, Oregon, Washington, and Colorado, they were now burning in Idaho, with thousands of people displaced and billions of dollars in property damage. Scientists in the Northeast discovered the Asian longhorned tick, an invasive species that received a special shout-out by experts for "transmission of exotic and local diseases that can make humans and animals seriously ill." Furthermore, the females could reproduce and lay eggs without mating. In case the Southeast felt left out, Hurricane Sally brought massive floodwaters and high winds to the Gulf Coast.

Most private schools in New York City remained open while public school was on again and off again and on again and off again. The soup kitchen at my church shares space with a school during the week, and on the first day back a solitary boy showed up for "super soccer." The coach played with him one-on-one, though I had an opportunity to make a few plays from my vegetable station when the ball flew past the net. The smile on this child's face and the shrieks of joy brightened up the afternoon for everyone packing meals, which had been much more fun in prepandemic days, before we became a socially distanced hazmat assembly line profusely sweating beneath masks, head coverings, and goggles.

Covid-19 continued to ravage the South and Midwest while Crazy Uncle Donald was holding cheek-by-jowl natural selection rallies in swing states across the country, and claiming the virus would be killed by "herd mentality." What could possibly go wrong? Liberal Supreme Court Justice Ruth Bader Ginsburg died on Friday, September 18, at age eighty-seven. In life, Bubbe Ruth was very much about dissent, however, she ascended this mortal coil on the eve of Rosh Hashanah, the Jewish New Year—a time for looking backward and forward, for introspection and repentance. Her demise was a shock to many, but uppermost was the fact that the current election might end up in the Supreme Court, and that Trump's court picks wanted to eliminate basic women's reproductive rights along with Obama's program for widespread health care.

The next morning the US officially surpassed 200,000 coronavirus deaths, although many medical experts believed that mark had been crossed several months prior, if one took into account all those lost who hadn't been tested or diagnosed. Every day there was a headline saying, "CDC Reverses Itself," but no one with an ounce of sense was paying attention to them anymore. The CDC, once respected around the world, now may as well have been called the Centers for Death and Chaos.

Next, Trump declared New York City an "anarchist jurisdiction," along with Portland and Seattle, in an attempt to withhold federal funding. They were a little late on this call since the closest we actually came to anarchy was back in March when seven million people were fighting over six rolls of toilet paper. The only chaos now, if you could call it that, was a population of feral-looking children getting their first haircut in seven months as they started in-person schooling. Still, Guv Dad was having none of it and took out his good stationery and wrote a poison pen letter ordering Crazy Uncle Donald and his pet Cheshire cat Attorney William Barr to knock it off or else. . ..

When I'm sometimes asked "When will there be enough [women on the Supreme Court]?" and I say "When there are nine," people are shocked. But there'd been nine men, and nobody's ever raised a question about that.

—RUTH BADER GINSBURG

Chapter 24

Blue State Blues

The first presidential debate was its own *Saturday Night Live* sketch with Trump constantly interrupting his opponent Joe Biden and the moderator Mike Wallace. Once again, New Yorkers have known for decades that The Donald is a complete jerk, and were gobsmacked that much of the rest of the world was just finding this out.

Around one o'clock in the morning on Friday, October 2, Trump revealed that he and his wife Melania both had coronavirus. It seemed like an odd time to receive and report test results. Most people assumed Trump was lying about when he first suspected he was infected, and that he continued to attend rallies, fundraisers, and probably even a presidential debate with coronavirus. He had known that he'd been around others who had tested positive but chose to continue a busy schedule that involved interacting with thousands of people.

On Friday afternoon, directly after his beloved stock market closed, the President was airlifted to Walter Reed National Military Medical Center. Conflicting reports emerged about the President's condition from his doctors, the White House, and Patient Zero himself. We automatically assumed they were all lying. Several observers noted that the Russians surely had better information on the President's condition.

A dozen people who'd been around Trump also reported they had coronavirus, including several advisors and his campaign manager, plus three Republican senators, two of whom happened to be on the judiciary committee. It transpired that an event the previous Saturday to unveil Trump's choice of Supreme Court justice (to steal Ruth Bader Ginsburg's seat before her body was cold in Arlington Cemetery) had been a super-spreader event. Maskless supporters crowded together in the Rose Garden and there was a reception inside the White House where people hugged, kissed, spoke, and shook hands. Nominee Amy Coney Barrett's political positions were antediluvian for modern women, so we hypothesized that the virus in the air was the Revenge of Bubbe Ruth. Picture the ghostly Fruma-Sarah in *Fiddler on the Roof* rising from the grave during the nightmare scene to set everyone straight when it came to making bad decisions.

The following day, Trump's doctor admitted that he'd been misrepresenting the President's condition in order to keep our spirits up, the same way Trump discouraged mask wearing and social distancing, so we wouldn't panic, only die. As the President prepared to go joyriding outside Walter Reed Medical Center so he could wave at supporters and endanger the lives of all the people in the car with him, New York Mayor de Blasio announced that due to rising coronavirus cases, schools and businesses would be closing in local hotspots. Covid-19 was spiking in a number of places across the country, with the number of new cases the highest since August 14, and nine states breaking records.

The divorce rate was up 35 percent in the US, so it came as no surprise that Mom and Dad were fighting *again*. After de Blasio announced his decision to roll back nonessential business openings in virus hotspots in Brooklyn and Queens, Guv Dad responded, "No way." Then the Mayor tried to overrule him by saying, "Way!" And then . . . who gives a crap because Crazy Uncle Donald had checked himself out of the hospital, declared Covid to be no big deal, and removed his mask the second he was back at the Blight House, where about four people were testing positive every hour.

Crazy Uncle Donald, possibly tripping on steroids, was now speaking in tongues, saying that he probably caught coronavirus from Gold Star families, that it was "a blessing from God," that Democratic VP candidate Kamala Harris was a monster and a communist, and his political opponents past and present must be prosecuted. Nana Nancy Pelosi was no longer talking about impeachment but the 25th Amendment, which is civics-speak for the people in white coats coming to take him away. Cue up *One Flew Over the Cuckoo's Nest* and Dale Harding's comment to McMurphy: "Never before did I realize that mental illness could have the aspect of power, *power*. Think of it: perhaps the more insane a man is, the more powerful he could become. Hitler an example. Fair makes the old brain reel, doesn't it? Food for thought there."

On Saturday, October 3, Crazy Uncle Donald held a rally on the White House lawn while he raved from the balcony how what he liked to call "The China Virus" was "disappearing"—while he was spreading it all over the place and cases were rising across the nation. Anyone who'd ever read a history book quickly pivoted from the Hitler parallels to Mussolini. Meantime, *Evita* parodies were arriving fast and furious, which included the political ad "Covita." So was talk of homicidal negligence on the part of the Coronavirus in Chief. At the same time, Hurricane Delta was slamming the Gulf Coast, which left over a half million residents without power. Hurricane Delta was the record-tying fourth storm of 2020 large enough to name to strike Louisiana, as well as the record-breaking tenth named storm to strike the United States in that year. Records kept being shattered every single day but none of them were the good kind.

In October there was a shortage of Mason jars because half the nation had suddenly become gardeners and were now harvesting enough produce to last a decade. A good thing since all we were hearing from medical experts was "Second Wave." Cases were on the rise throughout the Northeast, including New York City. First thoughts: 1) Six more months without pants; and 2) What was the toilet paper situation? But a sinking dread set in as we saw neighborhood businesses close for good and home-lessness markedly on the rise. Were we indeed returning to the crime and grime of the second half of the 20th century? Home sales in the surrounding suburbs contin-ued to skyrocket. Was the Big Apple rotting? It was an ominous sign when we turned to *Saturday Night Live* for some humor and mid-sketch a character broke the fourth wall to concur with the prevailing sentiment that we were going through a difficult time and did *not* know if things would be okay.

Political elections are a good deal like marriages.
There's no accounting for anyone's taste.

—WILL ROGERS

Chapter 25

Countdown to Chaos

As we ground through the Amy Coney Barrett hearings and the final three weeks of electioneering, I began to wonder why every time I looked at the TV news I saw grandparents running the country, grandparents hoping to run the country, and in some cases, great grandparents. Meantime, I wasn't seeing any eighty-year-olds, or even seventy-year-olds, for that matter, flying commercial aircraft, delivering babies, or commanding troops in battle. Not to sound ageist, but I know for a fact that when my relatives got to be seventy-seven they ran some errands in the morning, went for a drive in the afternoon, had a bowl of soup, and then settled in for *The Lawrence Welk Show* and *Murder, She Wrote*. They weren't thinking it was a good idea to run a large enterprise, or make decisions for people sixty years their junior, who'd be stuck with the consequences for generations to come. Put it this way, there's a reason that after your tenth birthday relatives start giving you cash on special occasions—you know what's better for you.

The day after the final presidential debate, and with the election less than two weeks away, the country saw at least 81,400 new coronavirus cases, the highest one-day total ever, and 225,000 Americans were dead from it. While the virus originally raged through New York, a port of entry for infected visitors from around the globe, rural (and Republican-governed) communities thought they might be immune. Far from it. The pandemic was exploding with a Third Wave of infections across the nation. Less populated areas were being particularly hard hit, while my own "anarchist jurisdiction" was now one of the safest places in the US, with a positivity rate of slightly over 1 percent. By contrast, South Dakota's positivity rate was thirty-five percent. (The state had been home to the Mount Rushmore fireworks party and the Sturgis motor-cycle rally, which brought half a million bikers together.) The red states weren't as big on wearing masks and social distancing because this interfered with their liberty to kill one another.

Trump rallies in swing states were leaving a trail of Covid clusters in their wake. The White House attempted to hide the fact that five aides to the Vice President, includ-ing his chief of staff, caught coronavirus while Pence (head of the Coronavirus Task Force) kept on campaigning. Hospitalizations and daily death tolls rose while experts warned that the worst was yet to come. Yet, the Presi-dent's chief of staff Mark Meadows (who recently held a maskless wedding for his daughter despite local officials urging against such gatherings) announced, "We're not going to control the pandemic." Why not? China (pop-ulation 1.39 billion) had 15 new cases on October 24, 2020, while we (population 332 million) had over 79,000 new cases. South Korea (population 55 million) had fewer than 500 deaths in total compared to our 225,000. Simultaneously, Dr. Fauci was saying that a nationwide mask mandate would be a good idea. So Trump signed an executive order . . . enabling him to fire Dr. Fauci. In other news, astronomers had discovered water and ice on the moon. Normally this would've received enormous coverage, however, with Earth exploding right beneath our feet there wasn't time for space exploration.

Things were expected to get a whole lot worse. Scientists around the country had been testing wastewater and found increasing levels of infection. This was a leading indicator, ahead of the number of people showing up at hospitals, and showed the country to be flush with coronavirus. Or, as city employee Rosa Inchausti in Tempe, AZ, so delicately put it, "The proof is in the poop."

Still, it appeared that Trump could still win the election. Democrats (and many former Republican voters) were desperate. A big story titled "Having Dementia Doesn't Mean You Can't Vote" ran in the Science section of *The New York Times*, and was given a more prominent position than "A Sea Lion's Last Chance: Brain Surgery." A week before the election, with sixty million people having already voted and polls predicting Biden would be the next president, and that Democrats could take back the Senate, ultra conservative Amy Coney Barrett was sworn into the Supreme Court by Republicans. There was good reason to fear that a six–three Republican-leaning court would help Trump steal the election. The way things were going, he would surely go down fighting and take us all with him.

With just four days until the election, polls suggested that Donald Trump would lose. However, they'd said the same thing last time when we thought for certain that Hillary Clinton was going to be the first female president.

This time, there was a new indictor to watch—Madame Tussaud's waxwork museum in Berlin wheeled its statue of Donald Trump out of the building and into a dumpster, thereby hinting at its expectations for the upcoming election.

Two days before the election, polls suggested that Joe Biden was leading, and Trump was planning to steal the election by calling it a done deal the moment he was ahead, before all the mail-in ballots had been tallied. Trump derided mail-in ballots as illegitimate, which was not only a lie but dangerous, since voting by mail was the best way to protect people from the plague that he'd failed to contain. Trump also had lawyers challenging hundreds of thousands of ballots in areas where Democrats dominated the electorate. If anyone doubted the "President" was counting on cheating, for proof they just had to look at the "non-scalable" fence being erected around the White House, and the 250 National Guardsman put on standby. Stores across the country were boarding up windows as if another hurricane was on the way, and hiring extra security, including the iconic Macy's in Herald Square and the Disney Store in Times Square.

In almost too good a coincidence, the news warned of a "feral swine bomb." Wild pigs—a hybrid of domestic breeds and the European wild boar, thereby creating a "super-pig"—were breeding exponentially and taking over the nation. In fact, some areas would soon have more pigs than people. The question was, according to *The Atlantic* magazine, "whether these regions can diffuse the pig bomb before it goes off." Many of us were wondering the same thing about the political landscape.

One day before the election, the parent company of Friendly's Restaurants filed for bankruptcy. This was disheartening on so many levels. For many of us, Friendly's was the "happy place" lodged in our childhood memories as the go-to spot for celebrating whenever something good happened. But also the place you went to heal after disappointment or loss, finding consolation in burgers, fries, hot fudge sundaes, and banana splits. It was where one always felt welcome in a mud-streaked Little League uniform with tear-stained cheeks, and mothers didn't worry about being denied service for wearing a house dress and scuffs. The affordable restaurant chain even kept English majors engaged, wondering what was the plural of Friendly's? Most of all, Friendly's symbolized an era before the best minds of my generation were destroyed by student loans.

The ignorance of one voter in a
democracy impairs the security of all.
—JOHN F. KENNEDY

Chapter 26

The Red and the Blue

On election day we kept hearing about "blue mirages" and "red mirages," however, the entire past four years felt like a black cloud. As President Trump insisted the pandemic was "rounding the corner," more than twenty states had set weekly case records for Covid-19 and more than forty states were seeing a pattern of growing infections. At least 93,500 cases were announced across the country the day before, the second-highest total of the pandemic to date. The nation was at nearly 8 percent unemployment and mourning the virus-related deaths of more than 231,000 people. Even places that weren't seeing a spike, such as New York, were experiencing deep economic distress along with pandemic fatigue and soaring mental health problems.

On election night there was a red tsunami and Trump went so far as to declare himself dictator before all the votes were counted. He threw a victory party with almost four hundred people packed into the White House East Room, funded by taxpayers. Meantime, the country surpassed 100,000 new daily cases of coronavirus for the first time, with steadily rising hospitalizations that threatened to overwhelm many health systems. Dems remained under the covers and only stopped gnawing their cuticles to reach for tequila and Twinkies. As for the Democratic losses within New York State, Guv Dad of course blamed those on Mayor Mom.

We awoke Thursday morning not knowing who was president, but there was more than a glimmer of hope that it could be former VP Joe Biden. Protests over vote counting erupted in cities around the country with community organizers yelling "count those votes" and heat-packing "militias" shouting "stop the count." Meantime, Trump was launching baseless lawsuits trying to stop legitimate ballots in blue urban areas from being counted.

The coronavirus hit another national high with 107,800 new infections. A North Dakota Republican businessman who won a spot in the state legislature had died a month earlier from Covid-19 at age fifty-five. North Dakota's politicians were on balance very much against supporting public safety measures, such as mask wearing in public and avoiding large gatherings to prevent the virus from spreading.

In Cincinnati, Charmaine McGuffey won the Hamilton County Sheriff's race to become its first female sheriff. McGuffey had worked her way up through the sheriff's department to the rank of major in 2013, and was then fired in 2017 by Sheriff Jim Neil, her opponent in the primary, whom she beat with a whopping 79 percent of the vote. McGuffey said she was terminated for being a whistleblower after exposing concerns about use of force in the department. She sued the sheriff's department and said that some within the department didn't like that she was an openly gay woman.

Hospitalizations and deaths were surging nationwide, and the situation was projected to get worse. The following day saw another US record—over 1,000 deaths for the fourth straight day and over 132,700 new cases. Add six more to that—the president's chief of staff Mark Meadows tested positive for coronavirus, after spending the past eight months very publicly playing down the virus, in addition to five other aides. They were instructed to keep it a secret.

Mental health problems were exploding as people had long passed their breaking points—everyone from toddlers to seniors were angry, frazzled, depressed, and fatigued by the pandemic. Head injuries were on the rise, mostly a result of falls. An increase in domestic violence was being called "a pandemic within a pandemic." My mom said that when she accidentally dropped her crossword puzzle book, she screamed and wanted to murder someone. The call to legalize marijuana and other recreational drugs in New York State had reached record volume. White masks were turning to black masks. People were tired of all the precautions and started to forego them altogether out of exhaustion and frustration.

Ballots were still being counted in Alaska, Arizona, Georgia, North Carolina, Pennsylvania, and Nevada. Drip, drip, drip, drip . . . Tuesday, Wednesday, Thursday, Friday. The words "Too close to call" rang in our ears. I had the hiccups for five straight days. Protests both for and against continuing to count the votes escalated. People were arrested crossing state lines with guns on their way to places where the count was close. Philadelphia's protester standoff evolved into a battle of the bands and a street dance party. Trump supporters favored Led Zeppelin and Bruce Springsteen (which I doubt the liberal Boss appreciated, especially considering he'd narrated an ad for Biden), while the Biden camp blasted rap and hip hop (which I'm not sure Grandpa Joe enjoyed, considering he was a self-proclaimed Frank Sinatra and Ray Charles fan, and turning seventy-eight in two weeks). On the bright side, there wasn't any band-on-band violence, and the whole affair could be managed by police on bicycles keeping the two camps apart.

By Friday it became clear that Biden was the winner, but the media seemed reluctant to call the race. Were they afraid of losing all their viewers and readership once the Trump circus left town? More likely they were afraid that Trump would sue them all.

Saturday, November 7, was an unseasonably warm November day. Just before 11:30 a.m. I was walking to the supermarket when the drivers of cars, trucks, and even city buses began honking their horns. I looked down at my phone and sure enough, Joe Biden and Kamala Harris had won. Along with the beep beep beep, pedestrians began a melody line of shouting and whoo-hooing. There was dancing, crying, leaping, laughing, and arm waving, sometimes all at once. There were bubbles, kazoos, and cow bells. We were masked but euphoric. Strangers addressed each other with cheers of joy and the most common line was, "I'd hug you if it weren't for the pandemic." Likewise, we all wanted to exhale, but it was too perilous.

Central Park, Broadway, Times Square, and other public spaces filled with spontaneous revelers and sociability. Jokes were also flying. "Queens Man Evicted" blared the *Queens Daily Eagle*. There were memes of the Statue of Liberty launching Donald into space using a slingshot made from a mask. Another presented him as a toddler who refused to give up his ball in preschool. The partying went on late into the night. A song titled "Fuck Donald Trump" hit #1 on iTunes.

Biden was victorious in both the electoral college and the popular vote by wide margins. However, Trump and his administration refused to accept defeat, and blocked Biden's transition team from accessing funds. Meantime, the Senate majority would remain undecided until two January runoffs in Georgia. In Covid news, the US surpassed 10 million cases while experts warned the country was entering a worse phase—there was a worse phase?

Secretary of Housing and Urban Development Ben Carson tested positive for coronavirus a few days after attending the White House election night super-spreader party. Carson was a neurosurgeon and another official who regularly attended indoor events without wearing a mask or social distancing. At least half a dozen other Trump staffers tested positive shortly afterward. With Trump's extensive traveling for rallies around the country, and golfing at his hotels, over a hundred secret service agents had Covid-19, or else were in quarantine after being exposed.

Cases kept rising. More than 11 million Americans had been infected with the coronavirus and over 250,000 had died. The country was suffering in a million different ways. North Dakota told nurses to continue working if they were infected but asymptomatic. The Nurses Association had something to say about that. So did my mother the RN—"stupid is as stupid does." Hospitals were triaging again—deciding who would get care and who would not—since there wasn't enough to go around.

Trump was on a golf course throwing a tantrum and tweeting how he'd been robbed, despite losing the election by over 7 million popular votes, and 306 to 232 in the electoral college. The Toddler in Chief decided to convince everyone that it was rigged and he'd actually won. I couldn't help but sense that our recent cultural shift from having winners and losers to everyone getting an A and a participation trophy had suddenly backfired.

There are certain queer times and occasions in this strange mixed affair we call life when a man takes this whole universe for a vast practical joke, though the wit thereof he but dimly discerns, and more than suspects that the joke is at nobody's expense but his own.

—HERMAN MELVILLE,

Chapter 27

Turkey For Two

New York City schools closed down again on Wednesday, November 18, despite attempting to hang on until Thanksgiving the following week. Staten Island reopened its emergency field hospital. Rates were rising in every single state plus Washington, DC, and the disease was killing at least one American every minute of the day. No matter what you wanted for Christmas, chances were pretty good you'd get Covid. Instead of looking forward to holiday festivities, Dr. Anthony Fauci told Americans to expect a "surge upon a surge."

Thanksgiving was mostly canceled. Word was that if you gathered for turkey and stuffing in November you'd gather for a wake and funeral in December. I had several friends in large families who were planning "secret

Thanksgivings" with just a few of their favorite family members. Some succeeded while several were busted. One morning TV show suggested that we email one another recipes instead. How fun! None other than Amazon.com rescued the holiday from being a complete wipeout by announcing that it would start selling prescription drugs online. Bring on the Prozac pie and Klonopin canes and wake me when it's 2021.

Trump's family decamped to Camp David in Maryland to expose drivers, secret service, and the staff there to Covid-19. After Thanksgiving it was discovered that many politicians, both Republican and Democrat, who'd advised constituents to cancel their own holiday plans, jetted off to visit family or for a vacation in Mexico. Some were outed by telltale signs in their Zoom screen backgrounds. The news wasn't welcome by those who'd canceled plans with loved ones at the last minute, like my friend Mary, and were left with a twenty-pound bird in the fridge. A round of what had become known as "Covid shaming" followed, with apologies from several politicians who were caught, but without pecan pie we weren't in a forgiving frame of mind.

Everyone agreed it was going to be a long, dark winter. Netflix showed a series called *The Queen's Gambit* about a chess prodigy, so everyone decided to play the game and stores immediately sold out of chess sets. *The New York Times* Style section ran a half-page article on how to make your own chess set at home, which included directions for an origami version with cats and dogs. If the following week Netflix had featured a program on woodworking, I suppose 300 million of us would've started building birdhouses.

I doubt I was alone in hoping that the four-year barrage of crazy news was over. However, in addition to Republicans trying to overturn the results of a free and fair election with definitive results, there was now a vaccine dispute. In the midst of infections rising at alarming rates, and threats of another lockdown, Pfizer announced they'd created a vaccine that was over 90 percent effect against coronavirus. The Trump administration immediately took credit for it, and the CEO of Pfizer announced that the Trump White House had *nothing* to do with their Covid-19 vaccine. Next, Trump threatened that everyone except New York State would get the vaccine. However, we knew that Gov Dad would have Crazy Uncle Donny fitted with cement overshoes and sleeping with the fishes before that happened. Our money was on the elected official *without* the gold toilets.

Crushed dreams, two canceled book tours, and a Third Wave of coronavirus forced me to finally tackle *Moby Dick* in an effort to process the endless barrage of bad karma. The pandemic likewise felt like a monster on the horizon—some bewildering mix of evil, nature, and fate. And the fact that a humpback whale was spotted near the Statue of Liberty in New York Harbor felt like a sign from the universe. Still, it wasn't an easy read—our attention spans have shortened considerably since 1851—and the title character doesn't show up until page 463 of a 486-page book. Furthermore, for a work touted as "the great American novel," there weren't any women in it, and there wasn't much America either, for that matter.

Another reason I felt beholden to finish what I'd started forty years earlier (by start I mean that I'd read halfway through the first page), is that Herman Melville had been a member of my church. Like most us, Melville came to Unitarianism (we weren't Unitarian Universalists until a 1961 merger), after a lifelong struggle with religion. Unitarianism has often been the last stop prior to forgoing organized religion altogether in favor of Sunday brunch.

Crazy story—for 120 years Melville scholars assumed that the author of *Moby Dick* had adhered to his Calvinist mother's faith. However, when Unitarian Universalist minister Walter Donald Kring was researching church history at All Souls in Manhattan, he discovered Melville's signature in the membership book. Not only that, Rev. Kring found letters suggesting a kidnapping plot! It transpired that in 1867 Melville's wife Elizabeth had sought advice from the Unitarian church's minister at that time, Rev. Henry Whitney Bellows, about leaving her husband. And one of them proposed a staged abduction in which Mrs. Melville, seemingly against her will, would be taken from her Manhattan home and spirited away to live with her half-brother in Boston. However, Rev. Bellows's lawyer Samuel Shaw (also Mrs. Melville's half-brother) said that he did not think a feigned kidnapping was a good idea. Four months later, the Melville's eighteen-year-old son Malcom died of a self-inflicted gunshot.

Rev. Kring had another brush with celebrity several years later. In May of 1977, he was asked to conduct a memorial service for famous movie star Joan Crawford at All Souls Church. Crawford was not a Unitarian Universalist, but in fact a Christian Scientist, and they don't believe in medical science or funerals. However, the actress was married to the chairman of PepsiCo and had been a board member of the company since her husband's death, so it was decided that a traditional sendoff was in order. The arrangements were made with PepsiCo's PR department and Crawford's daughter Christina, who'd just been informed she was disinherited along with her brother Christopher "for reasons well known to them." In attendance were longtime friend Myrna Loy and costars Geraldine Brooks and Cliff Robertson, who gave eulogies. Crawford's good friend Pearl Bailey sang the hymn "He'll Understand." In November 1978, Christina Crawford published *Mommie Dearest*, which contained allegations that her late adoptive mother had chosen fame over parenthood and was emotionally and physically abusive to Christina and her brother Christopher. *Mommie Dearest* became a best-seller and was made into a 1981 movie starring Faye Dunaway as Crawford.

"We'll never survive!"
"Nonsense. You're only saying that
because no one ever has."
—WILLIAM GOLDMAN,

Chapter 28

Dancing into the Abyss

Several vaccines were on the way, but a lot of good that did us in the moment. Otherwise, the airwaves were overwhelmed by King Donald ranting that he'd won the election despite being trounced in both the electoral college and popular vote. Like a blundering cartoon villain, he became intent upon trying to overturn the results using all manner of ludicrous schemes. Simultaneously, he was firing enough people in high places to make us fear that a Keystone Kops Coup was in the offing.

Trump continued losing the legal cases his team put forth, and more often than not their "arguments" were shamed out of the courtroom. Still, his supporters not only agreed that the election was rigged but seemed genuinely flummoxed that a President who never cracked a 50 percent approval rating could possibly lose. Trump's lawyer Rudy Giuliani spluttered nonsense while dark brown liquid ran down both sides of his face and it was how I imagined a leaking colostomy bag might look. Finally, Michigan certified the election results (after several days of playing will they or won't they), and Pennsylvania soon followed. Moments later the Dow Jones Industrial Average reached 30,000 for the first time in history.

Instead of holiday gift lists, magazines printed ideas for cheering ourselves up. One was to read *Studies in Pessimism* by Arthur Schopenhauer, which questions how a wise man can live in a world which we all know is a jungle, and concludes that we may as well make the best of things since we're here. Meantime, Herman Melville informed me that it's time to go to sea when you have "November in your soul" and are drawn to "coffin shops" and "bring up the rear of every funeral." However, we'd recently learned the hard way that cruise ships weren't the best places to be during a pandemic.

On the bright side, vaccine news was coming fast and furious with more companies announcing they'd succeeded in developing the much hoped for magical inoculations. The vaccine monkey puzzle went into high gear. When would it arrive? Who would get it? Should you get it? Who would go first? Did people who'd had coronavirus need to get it? What about the anti-vaxxers? Reporters were following production the way NORAD tracks Santa's sleigh as it circles the globe. On Saturday, Nov. 28 at 6:12 p.m., an alert went out that the first doses of Pfizer's vaccine had been flown from Belgium to the US. This version needed to be stored at below freezing temperatures to maintain efficacy so perhaps it was headed for Buffalo.

No one I knew wanted to get into the weeds on vaccine science, but after reports of some testing "irregularities," as with everything else related to coronavirus, a research-it-yourself approach was required. Contradictory information was coming from all over the place, including but not limited to academic research teams, global pharmaceutical corporations, tabloid news stories, scam artist pitches, televangelists, startup labs created solely to vie for the prize, our own politicians, and government health officials. There were people dying in hospitals across the country from coronavirus who still insisted that it was a hoax due to all the misinformation they'd been fed. Thus, we were understandably skeptical, and I'd go so far as to say downright mistrustful, and thereby forced into the biotechnology phase of our journey, boning up on clinical trials, placebos, interim analysis, immune response, messenger RNA (mRNA), spike proteins, adjuvants, harmless bacteria, viral vector vaccines, repurposed vaccines, efficacy rates, side effects, cold chain, freezer farm, anaphylaxis, emergency use authorization, "self-replication" design, and FDA approval. One assumed that our next crash course would be in quantum mechanics and the uncertainty principle, or perhaps we'd skip right to catastrophe theory. When I was growing up it was good to have a friend with a pool, and now I could see that it was necessary to have a friend who had done really well in science classes, because I didn't know mitochondria from meatloaf.

In keeping with the last ten months of whiplash, Mayor de Blasio abruptly reopened public elementary schools ten days after closing them. Apparently, all the bitching about restaurants and bars being allowed to remain open had taken its toll, because if young children were going to be at home then parents definitely needed to be able to go out and drink. If the rise in day drinking at home wasn't proof enough, the anticipated baby boom turned out to be a baby bust because birthrates had actually declined while couples were confined together.

The weather grew colder by the day but people were determined to stay outside, where the virus was considered least likely to spread. City sidewalks were covered in colored chalk and hopscotch boards, which I hadn't seen since the invention of the first Sony PlayStation and cherry crush vaping juice. Jumping rope had come back into fashion so I was on the lookout for marbles, jacks, and hula hoops. Central Park had become an 840-acre picnic ground and one couldn't travel a few feet without wandering through birthday and anniversary celebrations. In a more unusual twist, the park was filled with dozens of musical groups that had played indoors professionally until the pandemic and were now busking. Parkgoers had taken to gathering around and dancing, alone and with partners. Those who preferred waltzing and tangoing were by Bethesda Fountain, a hip-hop group entertained foot traffic on the Mall, and a jug band had folks stomping and two-stepping by Belvedere Castle. Alongside the Delacorte Theater a lute player dressed in Shakespearean garb featured a sign reading: "Take A Troubadour Home To Dinner." Broadway had been shut down for almost a year, but the arts were like a spring running underneath the city, quick to bubble up between any cracks.

Still, there was something else different about the park, and despite having lived a block away for twenty-five years, I couldn't quite put my finger on it at first. Central Park has hundreds of dogs in it at all times of day throughout the year. But more canines were running loose without owners, or else out-of-breath owners running a hundred yards behind yelling to please come back. They sounded desperate as they alternatively threatened and cajoled and then outright begged their dogs to behave. I hazarded a guess that many new pet parents were discovering that online dog training tutorials are no substitute for real life experience.

The Pfizer vaccine was approved in the United Kingdom on December 2. Many of us were glued to a new installment of *The Crown* series on Netflix, and wondered if perhaps we could return to the fold after our little 245-year experiment in self-governance had gone horribly wrong. Trump was busy working on pardons for all the swampy cohorts who'd joined in the pursuit of monetizing government while demolishing democracy.

Mr. A calls me into his office and says he's got bad news and bad news, and which do I want first. I say the bad news.

—GEORGE SAUNDERS,

Chapter 29

What Comes After Red Alert?

P earl Harbor Day came and went without so much as a television show about Japan attacking our naval base in Honolulu. What was there to say when more people were dying *every single day* from Covid-19 than were killed in that bombing? Day after day records were shattered. More cases—almost 15 million in the US. More deaths—almost 3,000 every day. Televised "heat maps" had to change their color scheme since almost the entire country had turned bright red. Many small and large hospitals were overwhelmed. Since the beginning of the pandemic there'd been doctors and nurses crying for help on live TV and streaming video, but that had been in virus hotspots. Now the tears were flowing all across the country. Everyone knew someone who'd been killed by Covid.

It wasn't just doctors and nurses who were burned out, but lab technicians, ambulance drivers, social workers, nursing home staff, funeral directors, hospital chaplains, and priests delivering last rites. People who had never been to a food bank in their lives were waiting in line for hours to be able to put dinner on the table. Supermarkets near me were placing ice cream, baby food, laundry detergent, and many other products under lock and key due to the alarming rise in shoplifting. No government aid was forthcoming. The economy was the worst it'd been since the Great Depression. Congress dithered while America starved. And the President continued to launch frivolous lawsuits in an effort to have the Supreme Court disenfranchise millions of voters. Trump insisted that he'd never worked as hard as he had over the past month, only none of that work had been for the American people.

We were told to "prepare" for the worst public health emergency in history, as if we weren't already in it. Dr. Fauci went on national television and urged Americans to "hang on" because "help is on the way." Was he purposely using song lyrics to try and calm us down? Or had we finally run out of science? Perhaps nothing expressed calamity more than Buffalo public health officials warning people not to leave home even to watch a Bills football game at a friend's house due to "living room spread." (The Bills were 8-3 and leading their NFL division!)

Former and future presidents were volunteering to get inoculated on camera. However, if you were over fifty, it was reminiscent of the "swine flu snafu" in which President Ford was vaccinated on live television, and then three senior citizens promptly died after being vaccinated at the same clinic.

More wildfires raged in Southern California, amid strong Santa Ana winds, sending embers a mile ahead. Most of the state had shut down again due to a fierce resurgence in coronavirus. Power outages threatened the thousands who were hospitalized, including many on ventilators. Normally, fire season would be ending now, but nothing had been normal for quite some time.

Several Republicans were calling for a declaration of martial law and a new presidential election so this time we could get the "right" result. From my ninth grade global studies class, I think that's what's known as a "coup." The House of Representatives passed a sweeping reform bill to decriminalize marijuana at the federal level. Seeing as how stressed we all were, this felt more like a humane gesture, akin to putting down a suffering animal that had no quality of life or chance for recovery.

Rudy Giuliani was still racing around the country not wearing a mask, arguing in packed hearing rooms that Trump won the election, with every appearance more difficult to discern from a *Saturday Night Live* sketch. The erroneous claim that Trump won was now known in rational political and media circles as the Big Lie. At a court hearing in Michigan, Giuliani went so far as to suggest a woman remove *her* mask, and four days later he was hospitalized with coronavirus. His super-spreading antics also forced the Arizona legislature to close for a week and the Michigan House to cancel a voting session. The next day, King Donald's other attorney fighting to overturn the election, Jenna Ellis, also tested positive for Covid-19.

The UK and Russia had begun vaccinating their citizens while coronavirus numbers in the US continued to shatter records. With forty-four days left in his presidency, Trump was no longer showing up for work while completely ignoring the plague ravaging our nation. Many business owners were understandably frustrated and angry that politicians could make rules that would drive them into bankruptcy through prohibiting patronage by customers, especially when it came to bars and gyms. This was leading to an increasing number of legal battles, and in some cases, uprisings by devoted patrons and physical alterations with authorities.

Sunday, November 29 was the first day of Advent, the start of the four weeks leading up to Christmas, also known as the "time of waiting." We were exhausted from waiting. We'd been waiting and waiting and waiting.

Clarence! Clarence! Help me, Clarence. Get me back.
Get me back. I don't care what happens to me. Only
get me back to my wife and kids. Help me, Clarence,
please. Please! I want to live again. I want to live
again. I want to live again. . . . Please, God, let me
live again. [snow immediately begins falling again]
— GEORGE BAILEY IN

Chapter 30

Nothing Rhymes With Pandemic

The White House was planning at least twenty indoor holiday parties with more than fifty guests in defiance of guidance from their own health agencies. The CDC warned that nearly 20,000 Americans could die of Covid during Christmas week. Secretary of State Mike Pompeo had a real end-of-life celebration in the works for 900 guests. Massachusetts Republican party leader Tom Mountain said he caught Covid-19 at a White House Hanukkah party that broke all safety protocols. Mountain's family later tested positive and he wound up in the hospital, close to needing a ventilator. "I was one of the naysayers," he proclaimed. "I am no longer a naysayer."

Santa, the elves, and his reindeer were all deemed essential workers. However, that was directed at rooftop

Santa. Other Santas around the country spread corona-virus as they worked in malls, marched in parades, and visited children in enclosed settings. Merry Fucking Christmas, as my mother the community mental health nurse liked to say.

People were busy canceling holiday plans when at 9:20 p.m. on Friday night, December 11, we all looked up from watching reruns of *The West Wing* to examine our phone alerts, and it was Victory over Coronavirus Day! However, there wasn't as much excitement as one would think on VC day. That's because the Trump White House had threatened to fire the FDA commissioner if the Pfizer vaccine wasn't approved Friday night, because the President needed a win, and he wanted it immediately (since his court challenges to subvert the election were being rejected). Almost half the population didn't trust the vaccine to begin with, and this stunt only served to decrease confidence by another ten or twenty percent.

You'd think a vaccine for a plague killing thousands every day and locking the rest of us inside our homes would be enough excitement for one night. However, the chairman of the Texas Republican Party suggested seceding, and that all other "law-abiding" (aka bat crap crazy) states should join him in forming a new union. I'm just going to come right out and say what most northerners had been thinking the past four years—we should've let the south go back in 1860 when they wouldn't accept the election of Abraham Lincoln.

As it turned out, people would have additional time to contemplate getting the vaccine as a Nor'easter barreled up the Atlantic Coast, halted traffic, and closed anything that may have been opened. The big fight in New York City wasn't over the last pair of boots at Timberland, but whether public schools should be open (and use distance learning) or declare an old-fashioned snow day. It was logical to go remote because if there is an excess of snow days, time is tacked onto summer vacation, when we'd all presumably be vaccinated and kids could enjoy normal life again. But no one was in the mood for logic—kids wanted to go sledding, have snowball fights, and build snowpersons while parents wanted to be able to work without distraction, and one assumed that teachers would welcome a day of rest. But no, online school it was, and everyone was miserable. When Catholic schools closed in favor of a "traditional snow day," it was probably the best move for converting the masses since the miracle of the loaves and fishes.

During this double lockdown, internal White House memos were released showing that the Trump administration had been angling for "herd immunity" all along, and the scheme was always to infect millions of Americans with Covid-19 rather than push precautions while waiting for a vaccine. "Infants, kids, teens, young people, young adults, middle aged with no conditions etc. have zero to little risk . . . so we use them to develop herd . . . we want them infected . . ." science advisor Paul Alexander had written back on July 4, regarding his "plan" that would've led to more than two million deaths. Alexander had also argued that colleges should stay open to allow infections to spread, with no regard for the surrounding communities, which had seen huge spikes in caseloads. Marginalized groups had rightfully complained for decades about being used as guinea pigs, so now the rest of us knew what that felt like. Otherwise, the mass infection plan was working! It was a new day of records—highest daily number of new coronavirus cases (247,357) and hospitalizations (113,069) across the country, and the single deadliest day (3,656) since the pandemic began. It was also a certainty that many people with Covid had not been tested, thousands were sick at home, and many would die at home only to go straight to the morgue without ever being tested. As alarming as the official numbers sounded, they were undeniably low.

The race to vaccinate everyone sounded like one of those reality TV shows that features a contest in which people are given outlandish challenges with limited resources and enormous obstacles. I turned on the news to hear the sentence, "FEDEX will take the western half of the country while UPS takes the eastern half." Brexit was happening in Europe, which should've been huge news, but all we saw were delivery trucks being loaded with containers of vaccine. Still, the UK managed to win the PR contest by not only beating us to the rollout, but televising the second vaccine recipient whose real name was William Shakespeare.

People clamored to know when they could get the vaccine while many declared their opposition to it. I put my information into a computer algorithm and it showed a picture of a long line of people with an arrow saying YOU that pointed to the second person from the end of the line, before a young androgynous person dressed in a striped shirt and a backward baseball cap. Many states were distressed when they received fewer doses than promised and the Army General responsible for distribution apologized for "the miscommunication."

December 18 was another good news/bad news day on a mind-blowing scale. Another coronavirus vaccine had been authorized for emergency use, this one by Moderna. Yay! But then Homeland Security announced the discovery of a massive cyberattack on dozens of government agencies (including ones involving nukes), private companies, and critical infrastructure entities (read: power grids and water supply) by Trump's crony and number one condo investor, Sugar Vladdy Putin. It was said to be the worst hack in history and so scary that in addition to adding more water and beans to our stockpiles, people were considering taking a sledgehammer to their microwave ovens and flushing their Fitbits. Bread machines and skylight digital photo frames were put on notice. This was a lot to chew on, yet the *big news* was a Facebook video shared tens of thousands of times about a tracking microchip implanted in those who received vaccines. The story included manipulated footage of commentary by Bill and Melinda Gates and Chinese billionaire Jack Ma, who were all trying to *stop* Covid. Still, I'm not sure how much debunking should've been necessary since it's possible to track anyone who has a cell phone. Implanting microchips was so 1985. Invisible ink, anyone? How about some itching powder?

It transpired that the microchip conspiracy was insignificant when balanced against the Brazilian President Jair Bolsonaro's criticism of the Pfizer vaccine. He suggested that side effects could include women growing beards, people turning into crocodiles, and men speaking with effeminate voices, while making it clear that he wouldn't be vaccinated. Brazil (182,854) had the second-highest death toll in the world, only surpassed by the United States (311,073).

He HADN'T stopped Christmas from coming!
IT CAME! Somehow or other, it came just the same!
—DR. SEUSS,

Chapter 31

You're A Mean One, Mr. Trump

D ecember 21 is the darkest day of the year in the Northern Hemisphere. It'd be ironic overkill to receive dark news on such a day, but there it was: a new variant of coronavirus said to be 70 percent more infectious was spreading rapidly throughout the UK and heading westward—or more likely, had already landed in US cities. (It had.)

However, Trump was finished with the pandemic—"It just exceeded the amount of time he gave it," according to one advisor. When not playing golf, King Donald spent his time pardoning felonious friends and coconspirators and planning his coup for January 6 when Congress was supposed to overturn the election in his favor. Abetting him were the three stooges—pardoned felon and former national security advisor Michael Flynn, disgraced former mayor Rudy Giuliani, and conspiracy attorney Sidney Powell. To make matters worse, King Donald claimed the recent computer hack wasn't by his KGBFF Vlad Putin, but rather China. All this while raising millions from his supporters, much of which could be used however he wanted. The only other matter that appeared to be occupying Dear Leader was getting an airport named after himself. Informal polls placed Moscow at the top of the list.

Evangelical leader Pat Robertson had proclaimed that Trump was part of God's plan for America back in 2015. And as recently as two months prior said that God told him President Trump would win (and that after five years an asteroid would hit the earth and "maybe" bring "the end"). However, the founder of the Christian Broadcasting Network received a contradictory newsflash from the Almighty saying that a Trump presidency was no longer in God's plans, not for 2020 or 2024. There was nothing further about impending doom from the asteroid so I assumed we could still take that prediction to the bank. Although I felt bad for Christian churches trying to raise money for renovations since the obvious answer was: "Why bother?"

In reptilian news, the National Weather Service in Miami issued an alert for possible "falling iguanas" due to a polar front heading toward the Sunshine State. Because iguanas are cold-blooded, they slow down or become immobile when temperatures drop into the forties, and tumble from tree branches even though they aren't dead. Warm-blooded residents were advised to leave the iguanas alone since they "may feel threatened and bite once they warm up." As if there wasn't enough to worry about.

Despite the warnings and worry, the holidays came after all. A national puppy shortage resulted in Horgis, Shih-Poos, and Golden Rotties trading on the dark web in bitcoin alongside stolen credit card numbers, steroids, and cyber-arms. Every family I knew was baking six thousand

Christmas cookies, while the Unitarians ramped up production of gingerbread persons, and the largest commercial cookie producers, including Pepperidge Farms, warned of "supply constraints." My friend Mary baked cookies for her children and grandchildren based on her mother's recipes but ate the first few batches herself and had to begin again.

The nation was in the grips of an eggnog shortage while cases of chardonnay flew off the shelves as everyone dreamed of a white Christmas. Tree sales (both real and artificial) broke records—wildfires out West had greatly reduced inventory and Canada didn't have as many trees for export since many of their snowbirds remained home for the holidays. Package delivery services were overwhelmed as they attempted to deliver gifts on time, along with all the groceries and necessities still being purchased online by the housebound, plus the specialized containers of coronavirus vaccine. Septuagenarian Santas figured out how to Zoom from their basements while twice-checking Naughty and Nice lists via email and spreadsheets. There was no better way to end a cyberchat with an excited seven-year-old than to say he had to get back to the workshop and make sure that toy production was operating smoothly.

No one knew better than Santa that the must-have gift for kids that year was a Sony PlayStation 5 gaming console. Meantime, there was a shortage of antacid across the country, because the perfect gift for adults was a container of extra strength Tums and a bottle of Pepto Bismol. Intestinal troubles clearly appeared to be on the rise, and the makers of Grape-Nuts cereal begged agitated customers to be patient while they replenished supplies. After all, nothing says Merry Christmas like a box of high-fiber cereal with a big red bow around it.

On Christmas morning a bomb went off in downtown Nashville that sent debris and shattered glass into city streets, injured three people, forced evacuations, and shook windows for miles around. Before the blast an automated message from the RV containing the bomb issued a warning and played a recording of Petula Clark's 1964 hit "Downtown." At least forty businesses were damaged in the explosion and there were "possible human remains" discovered at the scene.

Millions of Americans were in danger of losing much-needed benefits, and Congress passed a $900 billion Covid relief package, but Trump refused to sign it. He played golf at his Florida resort while the country held its breath in collective limbo, or perhaps "purgatory" was the better word. On Christmas Day, state governors facing massive shortfalls and distressed constituents were described as being "downright apoplectic."

Everything about this Christmas felt upside-down, from masks as gifts to Zoom choirs. Christmas carols were a fraught issue to begin with among Unitarian Universalists. Suggest a chorus of "God Rest Ye Merry Gentlemen" and people wanted to expand gentlemen to include women, nonbinaries, nonconforming, transgenders, transexuals, gender neutrals, questioning, and the pangender. Meantime, "Do You Hear What I Hear?" raised issues about sensitivity to mental illness, especially paranoia and schizophrenia. And "Silent Night?" We'd had enough of those.

Expectations went all topsy-turvy. A friend had purchased presents for everyone in his family and was looking forward to Christmas Day when relatives would gather for hors d'oeuvres and cocktails at his place and exchange gifts. Being a retired teacher, he's comfortably off but certainly not well-to-do, and delighted in the congeniality, along with the presents. However, a sister-in-law told the family that my friend had everything he needed and didn't want gifts this year. A nephew arriving with a bottle of wine apologized saying that the wine "was not a present." My friend watched as everyone, including the woman who had said not to buy him anything, opened piles of gifts. Meantime, my church experienced a phone tree snafu. The plan was to contact anyone stranded home alone for the holidays who'd requested a phone call. However, due to the "reply all" button being hit on an organizational email, the Home Alones received fifty calls apiece from various well-intentioned congregants. As one deacon remarked afterward, "Well, that's what answering machines are good for."

Christmas came and went with King Donald refusing to sign the relief bill. Two critical unemployment programs lapsed and people shifted from holiday mode to survival mode. Law enforcement reported that the Nashville bomber had been a sixty-three-year-old man carrying out a suicide mission. Since this was 2020 it couldn't be an accident or terrorist attack—no, the perpetrator believed reptilians and lizard people controlled the earth and had altered human DNA. Perhaps the only thing *not* surprising about the whole episode was that neighbors referred to him as a "loner" and a "recluse." That said, he had a girlfriend. And last year she just happened to warn the Nashville police that her beau "was building bombs in the RV trailer at his residence." Whoopsie-daisy.

Don't worry. It's no good overthinking this.
Calendars are just scraps of paper.
Be patient. It will all work itself out.
—YOKO OGAWA,

Chapter 32

F2020

When it came to death and number of infections, December was the worst month since the pandemic began and 2020 the deadliest year in US history. We were in the midst of "a surge on top of a surge on top of a surge" according to experts. The day after Christmas a grim milestone was reached: 1 in 1,000 Americans had died from Covid-19 since the nation's first reported case back in late January.

Through Trump's "Operation Warp Speed" one hundred million vaccinations had initially been promised by the end of the year, which would cover 30 percent of the US population. The number was quickly revised to 20 percent. However, more delays made the actual figure less than one half of one percent of the population receiving their first injection (out of two) by January 1. Senior citizens in Florida wanting to get vaccinated lined up all night in the rain and cold in a way they hadn't since trying to purchase tickets for a Beatles concert back in 1965. At this rate, experts calculated it would take ten years to get the pandemic under control. Sure, it's a big country, but in 1947 New York City vaccinated five million people against smallpox in just two weeks, and instead of super-computers and databases and the Internet they had pencils and notebooks and newspapers.

After sufficiently adding to everyone's hardship and stress with his Covid aid delay shenanigans, King Donald finally signed the relief bill on December 28, which, in addition to delivering much needed help, avoided a government shutdown during a pandemic. Still, no matter your politics or finances, everyone agreed that 2020 had been *the worst year ever*. As news programs and magazines did their "in memoriam" segments highlighting the celebrities we'd lost over the past twelve months, I didn't recall most of them passing, whereas in most years I could've identified 95 percent. I sincerely hoped I'd soon be able to brag that I'd forgotten every horrible thing I *did* remember from 2020.

Dr. Fauci, who was known for telling the truth about the virus, warned that the worst was still to come! As if on cue, the new highly contagious Covid strain first discovered in the UK popped up in Colorado in a person who hadn't traveled. The following day the variant was found in California, also in someone who hadn't traveled outside of the country. This was particularly bad news since Los Angeles hospitals were already rationing care and turning away ambulances while the dreaded refrigerator trucks were parked outside funeral homes. Florida was next—a man in his twenties with no history of travel had the new variant of coronavirus.

At the last minute, Trump ditched his maskless New Year's Eve party at Mar-a-Lago, where at least five hundred followers had paid a reported four figures apiece to cluster together and kiss the Mafia Don's ring. Instead, he spent the evening back at the White House plotting his coup: summoning Americans to take to the streets on January 6 to protest Congress certifying the election in favor of the winner, Joe Biden. Trump encouraged violence, tweeting, "Be there, will be wild!" Then he could declare martial law and hold a sham election in which he'd be declared the "winner."

Most people stayed up on New Year's Eve, not to watch the virtual ball drop in Times Square (which many of us had the urge to smash like a piñata), but rather to make sure that 2020 was in fact over. If we were to rate the year on Yelp it would have surely received Zero Stars across the board. There were no resolutions; we'd already given up more than enough. Perhaps the *only* good thing about all the masking, washing, and staying inside or away from others was that hardly anyone had caught a cold.

The US had 4 percent of the world's population, but 20 percent of the world's Covid deaths. Adding insult to injury, the United States had dropped to number twenty-eight on the Social Progress Index, which collects fifty metrics of well-being that include safety, nutrition, discrimination, the environment, health, and education. Despite our immense wealth, military power, and institutions for higher learning, when it came to quality of life, we'd slipped from nineteenth in 2011, and looked more like a developing country with a tinpot dictator than a superpower. The poor US response to the coronavirus was expected to lower our standing even further in the next round. We were not number one. Or even number two or number three.

We have met the enemy and he is us.

—WALT KELLY

Chapter 33

We Will Survive?

The year 2021 began with a total of 20 million corona-virus cases in the US, at least double the number of any other country in the world, and 125,000 people were hospitalized with the illness. The UK announced its third national lockdown. When the kids at First Unitarian Universalist Church in Brooklyn shared their dreams for 2021, the little boy who said he hoped Covid would be over by February because "I only have one more month left in me" not only stole the service but pretty much spoke for everyone. Not even the minister could top that.

On January 4 the highly contagious form of the UK variant of Covid-19 was identified in New York. Officials scrambled to speed up the rate of vaccination while states continued to grapple with rollout "complications," and it was no surprise that Guv Dad and Mayor Mom were once again playing the blame game. Meantime, one pharmacist intentionally destroyed a batch in Wisconsin because of conspiracy theories, and firefighters across the country were rejecting the vaccine at an alarming rate. Thankfully the new vocabulary wasn't too rigorous—a "vaxxie" was a picture of yourself getting inoculated.

Every horror movie worth the price of admission has the monster appear one last time right near the end. On the day that Congress was to certify Biden's win, King Donald held an outdoor "Stop The Steal" *rally* on the White House Ellipse to inflame the cultists and at least twenty-one Republican lawmakers from around the country he'd summoned to DC. Rudy Giuliani exhorted the crowd, "Let's have trial by combat!" No dog whistle here, just a whistle more akin to a starter pistol. King Donald fulminated for an hour about how he'd won the election, saying, "We'll never concede" and "If you don't fight like hell, you're not going to have a country anymore." He basked in the roar of the angry mob shouting, "Fight for Trump!" and told them to march on Congress to "save our democracy." Was incitement to riot and calling for insurrection no longer a crime?

As we learned in high school, most tragedies have five acts—exposition, rising action, climax, falling action and denouement—where the final scenes feature the death of one or more characters. (Though one could argue that in the Trump Tragedy, over 360,000 Americans had already died so far.) And so our long national nightmare proceeded on the afternoon of January 6, 2021.

Inside the Capitol, Congress had started the task of confirming Biden as our next president, despite a large number of congressional Republicans trying to disenfranchise millions of Americans. The proceedings were disrupted when King Donald's frenzied subjects overran police and stormed the Capitol building. The mob had been given the green light from the Commander in Chief of the United States, and they were just following orders.

You didn't need security clearance, access to the dark web, or a Magic 8 Ball to know that an uncivil war had been in the offing, since it was planned in open view on social media. The US was officially a banana republic. High-ranking officials were ushered to safety while House and Senate members were placed in lockdown and told to shelter in place. The rest of us had been locked down for almost a year by now so welcome to our world.

Eight hundred rioters intent upon capturing and assassinating elected officials entered the Capitol building carrying crosses, signs, shields, fireworks, guns, metal pipes, hammers, crutches (?), baseball bats, bear spray, hockey sticks, climbing gear, bullhorns, floor plans, and zip ties. Many wore red Make America Great Again (MAGA) hats (but rarely face masks), QAnon conspiracy theorist icons, Norse and white supremacist symbols, face/ body paint, animal pelts, and military-style garb. Some preprinted shirts were emblazoned with MAGA CIVIL WAR JANUARY 6, 2021. There was a "Camp Auschwitz" hoodie, and apparel with the acronym 6MWE—a reference to Jews murdered in the Holocaust meaning "6 million wasn't enough." A far-right media personality nicknamed "Baked Alaska" who espoused Neo-Nazi conspiracy theories livestreamed himself participating in the mayhem. And no coup would be complete without the spear-carrying Q Shaman in his headdress of animal fur and horns.

The insurrectionists paraded Trump flags, Don't Tread On Me flags, Release The Kraken flags, Jesus 2020 flags, America First flags, Betsy Ross flags (idolizing a time when minorities had no power), Confederate flags (which had not made it that far north during the Civil War) and even pro-police flags. In fact, the only thing missing were bagpipes. Outside of the building, a large wooden gallows was erected with a bright orange noose dangling from its center, where the paramilitary mob apparently intended to lynch the vice president.

A bloody body was taken out on a stretcher. Windows were smashed, offices vandalized, and excrement left behind. Trump's army scaled walls outside and inside of the Capitol building. Cameras captured trespassers roaming the marble halls of the Rotunda looking as if they were at a house party, smoking cigarettes, taking videos, and posing for pictures. They stole "souvenirs" from congressional offices, including laptops containing national security information, and left messages. "Murder the Media" was carved into a door. The chaos and ransacking went on for four hours. Some Capitol Police were making mall cops look like superheroes. Furthermore, several appeared to be palsy-walsy with the invaders, and you could imagine them all meeting at the bar later, like trial lawyers on opposing sides who are good buddies outside the court room.

Members of Congress sat on the floor and put on gas masks while the chaplain recited a prayer. As the hours dragged on one wondered why the invading mob wasn't being stopped with force. Why were they able to exit the building with no consequences? Why weren't the thousands out front being dispersed? Where were the tanks, rubber bullets, pepper balls, riot shields, tasers, handcuffs, batons, prisoner vans, and choppers that had been used on the largely peaceful Black Lives Matters protesters last June? These insurrectionists were white, and it was impossible not to imagine how the scene would have looked had they been another color or Muslim. Legions of TV viewers couldn't help but wonder how a rioter can get shot for looting a Victoria's Secret—but not for trashing the Speaker of the House's office? Perhaps some invaders didn't worry about apprehension because they were off-duty cops and retired military personnel from around the country. Indeed, few were being arrested.

Who was in charge? *What* the hell was going on? The White Supremacist in Chief was watching TV in the White House, cheering on his MAGA army, with no interest in stopping them or even saving his Veep from public execution. Two pipe bombs along with a cooler of Molotov cocktails were found near the Capitol building. Trump-driven insurgents also gathered at state buildings around the country, in some cases prompting evacuations and law enforcement mobilization. It certainly didn't help that many people had been stuck inside playing *Mortal Kombat* over the past twelve months.

When King Donald finally released a videotape, it was his arsonist/fireman routine, telling rioters to go home while fomenting their grievances by reinforcing the fraud fantasy. Trump sent his mob a Twitter valentine saying, "You're very special. We love you."

Order was eventually restored and our flag was still there, but it had been a white-knuckler. Five people died, including a Capitol police officer, and hundreds were injured. We always said that it can't happen here, yet it just had, or at least it almost did. In any event, the cuckoos had come home to roost.

The Inflamer in Chief's Twitter account was suspended for twelve hours while Facebook and Instagram cut him off until the end of his term. Better late than never. However, Trump still had the nuclear launch codes. And we had multiple new vocabulary terms: fifth column, flex cuffs, bear spray, Three Percenters, deplatformed, asymmetrical polarization, and post worst-case scenario.

Congress reconvened and several Republicans still fought to overturn the election on behalf of the Traitor in

Chief. Biden was finally confirmed as the next President in the early hours of January 7. Next came the business of trying to track down all those who'd happily breached the Capitol and then gone out for a cheeseburger or back home to clean their weapons. Who would do that? It would be *our* job. Indeed, as if we weren't busy enough with the plague, everyone was supposed to check the riot videos and send the FBI names and addresses.

Many called for the resignation of Josh Hawley from Missouri, who'd been the first Republican senator to publicly support Trump's bogus challenge and then raised a fist to show protesters his approval shortly before the riots. My husband wanted the Ivy League–educated Hawley removed from Congress for saying "irregardless" in his speech on the Senate floor. That was not an America my spouse or most English majors wished to live in.

The day of the Capitol Coup also made history as the deadliest day of the pandemic with 3,775 reported deaths. Until the next day, when deaths topped 4,100. Citizens desperately hunting for the vaccine crashed websites and flooded phone lines of health departments across the country. Under Florida's "first come, first served" plan there was some walker-on-wheelchair violence among determined recipients. In Texas, a Harris County judge compared the vaccine appointment process to *The Hunger Games*. In New York, the vaccine was impossible to find, yet the city issued an "Urgent Warning" for people seventy-five and over. What, exactly, were the seniors supposed to do? My eighty-four-year-old mother received a letter that same day saying she would *not* be vaccinated soon because she resided in a retirement community and not a nursing home. The letter was missing the paragraph saying when and how she *would* be vaccinated. It should've just said, "Welcome to vaccine purgatory."

We heard stories of those who hadn't signed up for the vaccine and weren't yet eligible who managed to be in the right place at the right time. Public health workers stuck in a snowstorm on an Oregon highway walked from car to car asking stranded drivers if they'd like to be vaccinated on the spot before the doses expired. One man was so delighted that he pulled off his shirt and jumped out of the car. Clearly this wasn't New York City, because pandemic or no pandemic, strangers offering shots are not welcomed with open arms. Despite the vaccine shortage and paroxysms of uncertainty surrounding distribution, no matter what news channel you turned to, it repeatedly showed a needle going into an arm, which didn't make for happy viewing, whether you wanted the shot or not.

As if the week wasn't hair-raising enough, on Friday we were informed that *another* highly transmissible variant of the coronavirus was spreading in the US. Some were suffering from what was now termed "long Covid" or "post-Covid-19 syndrome" according to *The Lancet,* which involved lingering and recurring maladies for these "long-haulers." People hadn't been able to freely circulate in almost a year and the economy was in tatters. For the lowest paid workers, the unemployment rate was over 20 percent. Experts warned that there was an "unprecedented eviction tsunami" on the horizon.

The year hadn't gotten off to a great start. An Internet meme said: *I'd like to cancel my subscription to 2021. I've experienced the free 7-day trial and I'm not interested.*

i am running into a new year
and the old years blow back
like a wind
— LUCILLE CLIFTON

Chapter 34

Trump's Last Stand

The morning following the insurrection, Speaker of the House Nancy Pelosi secured the nuclear launch codes and I assume tucked them in her pocketbook between a tissue and some hard candies for safekeeping. Then Nana Nancy informed the Toddler King to resign and go to his room or she'd impeach him (again) and he'd be grounded forever. Economists were busy debating whether the markets would experience a "K-shaped recovery" or a "doom loop."

Trump was permanently banned from Twitter "due to the risk of further incitement of violence," while Facebook and Instagram updated their ban from the end of his term to indefinitely. Mad King Donald threw a Trumper Tantrum, tried at least five accounts to get back on, and said he wouldn't attend the inauguration, presumably so his rioters could run riot.

Schools started the lesson on current events discussing words that begin with "In"—Indoctrinated, Inflammatory, Insurrection, Indefensible, Injurious, Investigating, Inauguration, Inoculation—and Insanity.

The new US variant of coronavirus turned out to be a false alarm, yet still another reason not to trust anything that came from the White House Coronavirus Task Force, and really the White House in general. Still, the old variant was breaking records as we paid for all those who'd traveled over the holidays, and the next six weeks were supposed to be the worst to date. Not to sound repetitive, but *how could things be any worse?* First, it was discovered that during the Capitol riot, someone exposed everyone to coronavirus in the House of Representatives lockdown, where several Republicans refused to wear masks. At least five lawmakers were diagnosed with Covid in the days that followed. Then, limits on cremation in Los Angeles were suspended so the facilities could "deal with a backlog" caused by the soaring number of deaths. Finally, the National Guard troops crammed into the Capitol following the putsch had all the makings of a super-spreader event.

The Pennsylvania Convention Center in Philadelphia held a "mass vaccination event" as if a famous performer was in town. New York state set a single-day pandemic case record of 17,636 with 197 deaths—a toll not seen since the second week of May. Mayor Mom announced that 25,000 NYPD personnel were eligible to receive the vaccine and then Guv Dad publicly slapped him down an hour later. Guv Dad insisted that health workers and nursing homes were ahead of them. Mayor Mom appealed for the freedom to make the right choices for his part of the household. Guv Dad shot back, "I'm not going to pick police over teachers and firefighters and grandma and grandpa." The next day New York's Police Chief Dermot Shea tested positive for coronavirus. Thousands of NYPD personnel had tested positive for the coronavirus—six detectives, a police officer, and 40 civilian employees had died, including Transportation Chief William Morris.

The Trump administration hadn't created a federal program for the distribution of the coronavirus vaccine but rather left it up to now bankrupt states whose health care systems were completely overtaxed, some on the brink of collapse. Furthermore, when the federal government announced they'd begin releasing coronavirus vaccine doses held in reserve for second shots, no such reserves existed. Oops. And despite everything we'd heard about the hordes of "anti-vaxxers" out there, demand far outweighed supply. In footwear terms, it was the equivalent of the Air Jordan 11 "Concord" drop two days before Christmas 2011 when mobs tore down mall doors and within hours the coveted sneakers were selling online for $500.

To help book vaccinations for senior family members, I was navigating complex websites (that kept crashing and freezing) and phone banks with hours of hold time. After nineteen hours of relentless efforts, we finally succeeded in making appointments, but two days later we received notices saying they were canceled because the supply had run out. At the annual meeting (on Zoom) of a large organization, the only thing 278 people wanted to discuss was how to get the vaccine. The following day, at an outdoor brunch with a friend who was considering selling her house, an eightyish man approached the table and said, "I've been overhearing your conversation and it sounds like you know what's going on. How do I get the vaccine? My doctor can't tell me anything." Due to the complex storage requirements, physicians weren't administering vaccines, and so it didn't matter how good your doctor was or how much he or she liked you. This last bit particularly aggravated the wealthy and well-connected who were trying to game the system; one complained, "What the hell is a Wall Greens?" People heard the eligibility requirements for getting inoculated weren't as strict in Florida, and this opened a new branch of pandemic travel called "vaccine tourism." However, "vaccine tourists" weren't to be confused with "vaccine hunters" who lurked near distribution sights in the hopes that there'd be leftovers at the end of the day.

Obviously, there was no federal vaccination plan. Why weren't we seeing ads for people to become "vaccinators"? My mother went back to school for nursing when I was a kid and gave injections to an orange at the kitchen table. (Which I had to try and explain to friends who came over to watch *The Brady Bunch*.) It took her a few times to get the hang of it and shortly afterward she was giving hundreds of injections a week. When my friend used artificial insemination to have children, I gave her HCG trigger shots in the kitchen. I wasn't even given a lesson or video to watch—just a small piece of paper with a few suggested injection sites. It was simple enough, although I couldn't see myself ever becoming a heroin addict.

On Saturday, January 9, an Indonesian passenger jet carrying more than sixty people dropped out of the sky over the Java Sea minutes after taking off. Normally this would've consumed every news outlet for days, but instead received about three minutes of coverage. Trump was in his bunker while everyone debated whether he should resign, be removed from office by the 25th amendment, or undergo another impeachment. However, most of his supporters shrugged and remained loyal. They claimed to be engaged in a "spiritual battle," apparently for totalitarianism.

Five days after the Capitol riots there'd still been no address to inform and reassure the American people from the White House, FBI, Pentagon, Homeland Security, Justice Department, Capitol Police, or even the Mall of America. The Instigator in Chief had not resigned or been removed from office. However, businesses began severing ties with Trump. New York City ended contracts that included two ice rinks and the carousel in Central Park, plus a golf course in the Bronx. Once again, better late than never.

A week after the riot, the President still refused to resign, claiming he bore no responsibility for the attacks, and VP Pence declined to invoke the 25th amendment to remove his boss, and so the House proceeded with impeachment (again) for "incitement of insurrection." This was the first time in history a US president had been impeached more than once. It was a week for records. Coronavirus deaths reached a single day high of over 4,400 lives lost. There was a new "new variant" of the virus, this one on its way from South Africa, and this mutation was thought to be more impervious to the current vaccines. And then there was *another* one coming from Brazil.

Federal officials told Americans not to even think about attending the inauguration. DC residents were warned not to leave their homes except for emergencies—was it possible to double down on sheltering in place? Your best bet was to watch the ceremony online while simultaneously trying to find a vaccine appointment. With the inauguration five days away, every state capitol in the country was on high alert as threats of armed protests and mob violence continued to grow. My husband was decidedly unhappy when his beloved New York City Starbucks closed due to "planned protests," and began making noises about moving to super blue Hawaii.

Meantime, the deranged Prom King clung to the throne wearing his orange makeup and gold crown, even though it had lost its magic. Law enforcement officials warned us of violence by "domestic extremists" in all fifty states not just surrounding the inauguration, but "throughout 2021." Pretty much the only thing left for us was a giant squid attack. Computers were put to use updating wills.

Hell is truth seen too late.

—THOMAS HOBBES

Chapter 35

A.D.—After Donald

The old seasons of winter, spring, summer, and fall had been replaced by impeachment, coronavirus, protests, and election. Being January, it was time for another impeachment. Over the past twelve months the temperature had fluctuated from below zero to over one hundred and so had the mood. Due to ongoing threats of violence and insurrection from right-wing extremists, Washington, DC, and state capitols across the country resembled war zones, complete with an enormous law enforcement presence, security checkpoints, armored trucks, roadblocks, prison-style fences, razor wire, helicopters, and drones. Friends in DC were calling it Mad Max on the Mall. The added protection was costing beleaguered states a fortune they didn't have. New York experienced its deadliest day of the pandemic since the summer and there weren't any human or financial resources to spare—nor any emotional and mental energy left in our psychic well. We were completely tapped out.

A day before the inauguration a new Covid-19 variant discovered in Los Angeles was declared to be "less susceptible to the currently approved vaccines." And the United States passed 400,000 Covid deaths, nearly a year after the first confirmed death. The number was projected to hit 500,000 in February, and experts warned of another virus wave the following winter.

At noon on Wednesday, January 20, the Domestic Terrorist in Chief became a private citizen as most New Yorkers exhaled a collective primal scream. The Queens, New York, native absconded to Florida, where Palm Beach County was trying to end their lease with him, and where I assumed the final chapter would be Chapter 11. Be sure to exit the Trump Library through the grift shop.

Joseph R. Biden was sworn in as the forty-sixth president of the United State and the Marine Band triumphantly struck up "Hail to the Chief," but the better choice might have been "I Am Weary, Let Me Rest." Fortunately, there was only one new vocabulary term for our strained brains: "First Second Gentleman." Democrats Raphael Warnock and Jon Ossoff, having won their runoff Senate races in Georgia, were also sworn in, and Republicans no longer held the majority. Was our long national duck-and-cover drill finally over? One hoped never again to hear the T-word again, but as psychiatrists know all too well, you can never truly break up with a narcissist. *Death of a Salesman* is an oft-revived American classic.

Perhaps our country could benefit from rebranding. The Canadian mining town of Asbestos had recently changed its name to Val-des-Sources, meaning Valley of the Springs. How about the United States of Shaka? Shaka is the Hawaiian hand gesture made by extending your thumb and pinkie that generally symbolizes the "aloha spirit"—a feeling of gratitude, friendship, understanding, and solidarity. Drivers will often use it on the road when you let them in.

On Inauguration Day, at least 4,131 lives were lost to the pandemic in the US. Over the following weeks, access to the vaccines eventually became widespread, and there finally appeared to be light at the end of the tunnel; or was it a train coming directly at us, one might well ask based on recent events.

Ever so slowly, the survivors were able to resume living, and the clock could be heard to tick again. While walking down crowded city streets I *almost* felt like hugging everyone. An entire year had disappeared since the deadly virus landed in New York. We plunged ahead into a strange, altered landscape. We were no longer muted. The world had changed and so had we. It was as if we'd been through a war together, or at the very least an Ingmar Bergman film.

Upon the conclusion of a tragedy, the final step, at least in English class, is to locate the "hidden lesson." The fact of the matter was that politicians, many with degrees from Ivy League universities, had been manipulating Americans who needed help, mostly from the government, but in some cases, also from mental health professionals. These politicians had a great deal of assistance from news outlets and social media. "Anger" is from the Old Norse word *angr*, which means grief. It's not that big a step to the word *anguish*. And from there we need *action*.

Simultaneously, a number of church congregations had embraced a new commandment that apparently read: Love thy ally, kill thy opponent. And words have consequences, as our kindergarten teachers liked to say. Sometimes even deadly consequences. Add to that the old maxim that a lie gets halfway around the world before the truth has a chance to get its pants on.

During what will surely go down as the most chaotic twelve months in American history, we'd learned what we can live without, but it transpired that democracy was not on the list.

We'd also learned what we can live with, and that was a whole lot of crazy. We discovered that toilet paper doesn't go bad, but if not stored properly it can grow mold. We learned that outfits don't matter all that much, and the importance of elastic waistbands. In a world that valued managing time, we were suddenly forced to give more careful study to managing emotions. Though the days could seem monotonous, we realized that each one required a different blend of conversation, complaining, and compassion. Finally, many people got a year of "practice retirement" only to discover that it definitely was or was not for them.

Most parents realized that teachers should be paid a whole lot more. As a result of the pandemic, more undergraduates were heading to medical school, not unlike how *All The President's Men* excited a generation about investigative reporting, and *Bonfire of the Vanities* diverted students from dentistry to Wall Street. I assumed that some aspired to become zoonoticists, because what could be cooler to list as one's occupation than that!

Some things happen for a reason,
Others just come with the season.
—ANA CLAUDIA ANTUNES

Chapter 36

The End of an Error

Life goes on, as they say, except when it comes to shaking hands, restaurant buffets, salad bars, and blowing out birthday candles. And while the pandemic raged, scientists had discovered new information about Homo Sapiens and Neanderthals, who'd coexisted for a period of time. Ancient bones discovered in caves suggest that Neanderthals were larger and stronger than our ancestors. But they became extinct and Homo Sapiens survived, spread across the earth, and flourished. Anthropologists have long debated what caused this mysterious disappearance of the Neanderthals. Was it a plague? A famine? Were they defeated and slaughtered in an epic war? The most persuasive theory is that Homo Sapiens won the battle for survival because of their superior *brain power*. They applied their intellect to better cooperation and outmaneuvered the physically more powerful Neanderthals in the competition for survival.

On the subject of annihilations, half of all species had gone extinct over the past twenty years, and every time we lose a species, the world unravels just a little bit. Not just in those places, but everywhere. We've overexpanded, overharvested, overmined, and used up more than our fair share of resources. While we were battling with the pandemic, the West Coast had its worst fire season and the Atlantic its most active hurricane season. There were huge wildfires in the Amazon and the Arctic, and the last fully intact ice shelf collapsed in the Canadian Arctic.

Wildlife brings pleasure, and in some cases provides food, but it also ensures much-needed balance. We have pushed nature to the brink, on land, in the sky, and under the sea, and scientists estimate that life as we enjoy it may only be around for another two decades. If that's not a call to action then we might want to consider that 1) All species eventually go extinct; and 2) Humans are a species.

Humans are also the only animals who enter into show business. (And perhaps this explains why shark attacks are on the rise.) If you grew up in America before the computer age, a delirious excitement engulfed the populace when the circus came rolling into town. We were mesmerized by the big top tent, mammoth elephants, man-eating tigers, stilt walkers, acrobats on horseback, trapeze artists, whiteface clowns, and of course the bombastic ringmaster, who is charged with keeping the audience on the edge of their seats throughout the entire show. A sort of time warp occurred as locals gaped at death-defying acts and the "freaks" on display for their hideous deformities. Teachers, mail carriers, and gas station attendants enjoyed the raucous beer tent and a midway that beckoned with its bright lights, carnival barkers, and tempting games of chance (which were very much rigged against the player). We circled round and round on the carousel with its gaudy calliope music and the Ferris wheel launched us heavenward. (A rider from above once vomited into my mother's lap.)

Captivated townspeople stayed out late, and even skipped church to partake of the diversions as a devil-may-care attitude set in, even among the typically well-behaved. Reality had been suspended, while judgment and reason were replaced with temptations and false promises. Escapades and shenanigans ensued, as if everyone had been shot out of that human cannon, and occasionally resulted in a local signing on with the traveling performers. Then one morning we awoke to an empty lot littered with crushed beer cans and candy wrappers along with enormous piles of manure. It felt as if a collective phantasmagorical fever dream had abruptly broken.

My father was a folksinger, and when the circus wasn't in town, which was most of the time, he was our live entertainment. Accompanying himself on the guitar, Dad specialized in protest songs like "Where Have All the Flowers Gone" and "If I Had A Hammer" since Unitarian Universalists firmly believed that we could stop wars by singing in a round. Sometimes he'd play "Wasn't That a Time!" about launching deadly wars to save humanity, and I've always remembered the chorus:

> *Wasn't that a time, wasn't that a time*
> *A time to try the soul of man*
> *Wasn't that a terrible time?*

Dad's been gone nigh onto ten years, and I can honestly say that I'm glad he didn't live to see "President" Trump or the pandemic. However, throughout his four score years and two, Dad typed thousands of letters to various friends and relatives, and signed every single one "The Future Is Bright." Let's hope he's right.

The welfare of each of us is dependent
fundamentally upon the welfare of all of us.
—THEODORE ROOSEVELT, 26TH PRESIDENT, REPUBLICAN

Chapter 37

The Invisible Jigsaw Puzzle

I grew up among religious people. One Sunday the local parish priest announced that there are 813 different types of sins. He didn't go through them, but nonetheless everyone wanted that list. However, what I heard around my house on a daily basis was, "Life isn't fair, so get used to it." And if you played dodgeball as a child, you knew this was indeed a gospel of sorts.

Women in the West African Ashante tribe make pottery for cooking and storing food, whereas the Ashante men are responsible for woodworking. In the Hadza tribe, men hunt while women focus on raising vegetables. When I was a kid in the 1960s and 70s, women were responsible for cooking and cleaning, while men did lawn care and car repair. There were washerwomen and lunch ladies but no washermen or lunch gentlemen. There were garbage men and cable guys, but no garbage women or cable gals.

Societies have been based on the division of labor since time immemorial.

When we start school as young children, further sorting takes place, and numerous competitions are set into play. A teacher probably told you that life isn't a competition, at least aside from grades, and athletic ability, and spelling, and reading, and behavior, and college entrance, and careers, and wealth, and status. "Just do your best," we constantly hear, and "You're only in competition with yourself." On the other hand, if that were really true, wouldn't we just tell each other to give up?

Fortunately, we don't live in a world where someone must suffer for someone else to prosper. The blessing of modern civilization with centralized governments, as opposed to tribalism, is that there should be enough opportunity for all, even if we don't compete directly with one another. Still, one rarely loses the sense that there's a competition afoot. People dress up to win partners and jobs. We improve our credentials to be more marketable and secure. We feather our nests to make an impression.

Clearly, there's a reward system. How can some film actors make more than school teachers? Or a stockbroker earn more than a janitor? Or a supermodel clear ten times that of a pediatrician? We've recently been reminded of just how essential grocery store workers, fruit pickers, and truck drivers can be to our survival. To a large degree, it matters more how many people we *impact*, rather than what we do. Write an unpublished book and you're a nobody. Write *Harry Potter* and you're a world famous gazillionaire. Save a life and you're a small-town hero. Cure cancer and you're a legend. Get naked for one person and you may make them smile. Get naked for fifty million people and you could be the next social media star (or have your computer taken away by your children).

Most of us possess an innate sense of right and wrong. And we like that there are referees and judges and supervisors, at least when they're doing their jobs properly and with integrity. Play by the rules and win and get a trophy that is deserved; cheat and be penalized or disqualified. But reality can be messy. You studied hard but failed the exam. You worked hard but weren't promoted. You love him (and perhaps sent him a photo you thought he'd enjoy), but he doesn't return your calls. What if a colleague scored front row seats to *Hamilton* because his sister works as the stage manager? Meanwhile, all senior citizens, regardless of income, receive senior discounts.

Oftentimes, we need to take direction from people who are clearly *so* wrong—bosses, teachers, politicians, parents, or even our grown children. And this feels unfair because we have different priorities and points of view. Maybe they know something we don't, like the company will go out of business if an unpopular decision isn't taken. A parent is usually putting long-term health over short-term happiness, much like an adult child ordering around an older parent. Or, maybe they're just being idiots, as we suspected in the first place. A Calvin & Hobbes cartoon said, "The world isn't fair, Calvin," and Calvin responded, "I know Dad, but why isn't it ever unfair in my favor?" However we feel at the time, such actions aren't typically meant to be judgments on who we are. They're just a byproduct of being alive and living in society. Thus, our idea of fairness isn't actually obtainable, but rather a cloak for wishful thinking.

Imagine how crazy life would be if it were "fair" to everyone. Business enterprises would only fail if workers were bad. Sports teams would let anyone join and give them all a chance to play equally. I actually had a born-again Christian soccer coach who did this and we lost almost every game for four years, had low morale, and no scholarship offers. In my estimation, fairness has actually come a long way, especially when I see the diversity of news commentators today compared to when I was a kid, and certainly among those protesting for social justice. Even school cafeterias have more options. When I was in first grade your choice for lunch was, do you want to eat it or not. In the world of absolute fairness, relationships would only end when both partners passed away simultaneously.

Most of us have a sense of flexibility when it comes to justice or fairness, and I sincerely hope that Unitarian minister Theodore Parker was right about the long arc of the moral universe tending toward justice. Reverend Parker often wrote sermons with a loaded pistol on his desk because he had fugitive slaves in his home to protect.

Sometimes it's just a matter of adjusting our own internal reward system. Unitarian author Theodore Geisel, who is better known to his fans as Dr. Seuss, cleverly demonstrated how Sneetches with stars on their bellies thought they were the best, and looked down on Sneetches without stars. Then along came Sylvester McMonkey McBean with his star-on-star-off machines, who gives stars to the plain-bellied Sneetches until they're happy to look like their elite counterparts, but the original star-belly Sneetches are angry and have their stars removed. It's worth noting that along the way McBean gets wealthy off his machines. This continues back and forth until no one can remember who had what until an epiphany strikes— they are all really the same and can coexist. It's positively frightening to observe the similarities between this 1953 children's story and the 1994 Rwandan genocide.

Sometimes unfairness is intolerable, and it appears such a threshold might be in our DNA. Two capuchin monkeys were taught to hand over pebbles in exchange for cucumber slices. They were both happy with this deal. Then a researcher offered one monkey a better deal—a grape for a pebble. Monkeys love grapes, so this was a big hit, only now the monkey who received the cucumber slice hurled it back at the researcher. It is evident that monkeys care deeply about fairness; not just what they receive, but what others get. And so do their human cousins. A study to determine what factors caused most air rage incidents concluded that it's first-class cabins.

It feels unfair that property taxes determine the quality of local public schools such that areas with expensive homes offer by far the best educations. It feels unfair that people die from coronavirus—people we loved, but also people we never knew. It feels unfair that certain parts of the country have been hit so disproportionately. New Yorkers feel it was especially unfair to have so many Covid cases after receiving the brunt of the 9/11 terrorist attacks. And it feels unfair that people of color have been impacted at a much higher rate. Because to be human is to be part of another entity that we call society or community. To paraphrase English poet John Donne, who survived two major plagues: *No person is an island. Any person's death diminishes me, because I am involved in Humankind.*

Two millennia ago, Aristotle said that fairness meant that each person receives what he or she deserves, and this is still a bedrock of our legal system. Inequality not only feels unfair, but it can also destabilize society. In America, the top 1 percent own more than the bottom 90 percent. The annual Wall Street bonus pool is more than the annual year-round earnings of all Americans working full-time at minimum wage. A well-known example of inequality is the amount that players on professional sports teams are paid. One assumes this practice leads to better performance and more wins. However, studies show the exact opposite is true—teams with greater pay equity did much better, perhaps because they felt more cohesion. Even more surprising, the *stars* did better on teams with flatter compensation schemes, as inequality seemed to undercut the superstars it was meant to foster.

There is a parallel when it comes to societal issues. Countries with the widest gaps in income, including the United States, generally experience worse health, more homicides, and more homelessness. In a study of people in over forty countries, liberals said CEOs should be paid four times as much as the average worker, while conservatives said five times as much. However, the average CEO at America's largest public companies earns about 350 times as much as the average worker.

Inequality has also been shown to make us more apt to believe weird ideas and superstitions. And more likely to cling to camps divided not only by income, but race and ideology, while our trust in each other erodes, including among family members, friends, and neighbors. This third category—neighbors—worries me the most. My hometown of Buffalo is nicknamed the "City of Good Neighbors." You can translate that to mean we have more Midwestern "nice" than East Coast haste. Or you can look at Western New York, a place with a historically harsh climate and residents spread out on farms, where, in the event of an emergency, it wasn't the police or fire department or ambulance or dog catcher who was going to save your life or your child's life. It was your neighbor. Indeed, everyone was a First Responder. And whether you thought them to be a bit odd, or didn't agree with their religion or politics, you made it a point to get along.

Our first instinct is to lay divisiveness at the feet of those in power. Essayist Suzy Kassem writes, "When people can get away with crimes just because they are wealthy or have the right connections, the scales are tipped against fairness and equality. The weight of corruption then becomes so heavy that it creates a dent that forces the world to become slanted, so much so—that justice just slips off." However, these are symptoms and not root causes. Digging deeper, I think we'll find that until we confront and remedy unfairness, and replace disparity with opportunity, we will continue to be a stressed-out society, making us all less healthy and less happy. This is not an easy task, especially when we consider that most factors behind inequality—such as gender norms, class, and slavery—have been in operation for thousands of years.

We might also consider how we're often unwilling to tolerate unfairness toward ourselves, while not worrying quite as much when the unfairness is directed at others. Transcendentalism began as a movement largely among young Unitarian ministers and lay leaders determined to bring about a moral and spiritual renewal within their churches. They welcomed the assessment by Immanuel Kant that there are transcendent ideas that shape our sense perceptions. In ethics, Kant's "categorical imperative" forbade forming a moral norm for others that one would not want imposed on one's self. This would have implications for racial, gender, and social justice, along with personal spiritual practice, and continues to do so. Most of us are concerned about how the world should work. And we do have some control over the reward system—we can buy fair trade food, support causes that promote fairness, make our voices heard, and of course vote in every single election.

In 1911, Manhattan's Greenwich Village was a hamlet of progressivism within a less open-minded city, state, and country that condoned lynchings, didn't let women vote, and where miscegenation, homosexuality, and crossdressing were punishable by law. Greenwich Village harbored inter-racial couples, same-sex couples, throuples, political radicals, artists painting and penning works considered immoral, and birth control advocates who would've been arrested or worse elsewhere.

Into this motley multitude moved a Lebanese-born artist and mystical writer who penned a slim volume of poetry that sold a thousand copies when it was published in 1923. *The Prophet* is now one of the best-selling books in history, with over a hundred million copies printed in almost fifty different languages. In its pages Kahlil Gibran writes: "You have been told that, even like a chain, you are as weak as your weakest link. This is but half the truth. You are also as strong as your strongest link."

We must never forget that we are not alone, that we have sisters and brothers and others all across the country deeply feeling the need for change. We are also as strong as our strongest links. Just because inequality is the norm doesn't mean it has to be inevitable. Fairness can be difficult to define, and therefore it's easy to look away, so let's just say that fairness is what's left over when unfairness is abolished.

THE END

About the Author

L aura Pedersen is the author of 5 plays and 18 books including the award-winning *Buffalo Gal* and *Life in New York: How I Learned to Love Squeegee Men, Token Suckers, Trash Twisters, and Subway Sharks.* She is President of the Authors Guild Foundation. Find more on Facebook/Laura Pedersen Writer.

Author photo © Denise Winters

Made in the USA
Middletown, DE
21 May 2021

39663874R00128